TRAINED IN
Divine Love

Nayaswami Anandi.

TRAINED IN
Divine Love

My Life with Paramhansa Yogananda
and Swami Kriyananda

By Nayaswami Anandi

CRYSTAL CLARITY PUBLISHERS   Commerce, California

Crystal Clarity Publishers
crystalclarity.com | clarity@crystalclarity.com
1123 Goodrich Blvd. | Commerce, California
800.424.1055

ISBN   978-1-56589-064-0 (print)
ISBN   978-1-56589-581-2 (e-book)
Library of Congress Cataloging-in-Publication Data available

Cover design by Tejindra Scott Tully
Interior design and layout by Michele Madhavi Molloy

The *Joy Is Within You* symbol is registered by Ananda Church of Self-Realization in Nevada County, California.

To sincere seekers, whatever their chosen path

Sunday service at Ananda Village's Yogananda Amphitheater.
Left to right: Devi, Jyotish, Bharat, Swamiji, Anandi, and Jaya.

Contents

Foreword

ANANDI AND I MET for the first time one hot summer morning in 1971, soon after she had arrived at Ananda Village. We were working together trying to get a field of clay-hard soil ready for planting. This apparent stranger toiling beside me quietly commented to herself, "This is a very existential experience. It's like raking a sidewalk." Those few words triggered a profound recognition within me — an awakening of an old, dear friendship.

We began talking and soon discovered an astonishing connection. It turned out that we'd grown up just one mile from each other in St. Louis, Missouri — thousands of miles from where we now stood — but had never met.

Such was our destiny that it wasn't until that bright summer morning in a barren field in Northern California that a lifelong friendship took root. Over the next fifty years it flowered, ever a source of mutual joy, support, and inspiration.

The empty field in which we first met was a fitting symbol for the lifelong journey we traveled together. Since we were both new then to the spiritual path, our consciousness was like untended soil, overgrown with weeds of worldly thinking. But we kept at it, and just as that field grew in time into a fertile garden, our consciousness changed and bore spiritual fruit as the years went by.

The outer harvest of Anandi's spiritual efforts was an abundant, never-ending crop of divine friendship, wisdom, kindness, and guidance which she shared selflessly with everyone she met. What a joy it was to see her engaged in animated conversation with some new guest at The Expanding Light. For anyone's guess, they were the best of friends. Return visitors often said that they came back just to talk with her.

Her devoted husband, Bharat Cornell, describes in his introduction how, after Anandi's passing in 2022, he found a manuscript sharing her personal journey: *Trained in Divine Love—My Life with Paramhansa Yogananda and Swami Kriyananda*. Though Anandi and I had been close for many years, when I read her words it struck me powerfully how little I had really known her. Anandi's true self was expressed fully only in her relationship to God and Guru.

She describes how God trained, disciplined, and guided her in her quest to find Him. Her deep longing for divine union is reflected in the lyrics of Swami Kriyananda's beautiful song, "God's Call Within":

Listen! Listen!
Whispering within your soul:
Hints of laughter, hints of joy;
Sweet songs of sadness, of quenchless yearning
For the Light,
For My love, your true home.

Everyone who knew Nayaswami Anandi felt great sadness and loss at her passing. Yet as time has passed, and now as we read in this book about how hard she labored in the fields for God, we can also rejoice that we were blessed to share a life together with her.

Jesus Christ said, "The harvest is plentiful, but the laborers are few." Whether you knew her or not, I know Anandi would want to share her story with you, in the hope that, drawing encouragement from the "plentiful harvest" she found in living for God, you too might become such a "laborer" and partake of that harvest.

Nayaswami Devi
June 19, 2023
Ananda Village

Swami Kriyananda (1926-2013).

About This Book

FOR FIFTY YEARS, Nayaswami Anandi was a deeply devoted disciple of Paramhansa Yogananda, and of his beloved disciple, Swami Kriyananda.* To everyone she met, Anandi was a beautiful channel of divine love; her life's quest was to reciprocate and to express the pure love she received in such abundance from Sri Yogananda (1893-1952) and from Swamiji (1926-2013).

Anandi left her body on January 30, 2022. The physical cause was angiosarcoma, a rare and aggressive cancer. For the previous forty-one years she and I shared a joyful soul marriage and life of service, often focused on lecturing and writing. At the time of her passing I did not remember that she had left behind an unfinished manuscript describing her vibrant inner life with Paramhansa Yogananda and Swami Kriyananda. Her passing brought so many changes to my life that I had forgotten its existence.

* Paramhansa Yogananda is a revered world teacher, recognized as one of the greatest emissaries to the West of India's ancient wisdom; Swami Kriyananda is one of Yogananda's foremost disciples, trained by the Master to spread his teachings throughout the world. In 1968, Swamiji founded Ananda Village (which he later renamed Ananda World Brotherhood Village) in the Sierra foothills of Northern California. Ananda is a spiritual community dedicated to living and sharing the universal ideals and practices of Yogananda.

Four months after her passing, I had a dream of a book hovering above my forehead, absorbing my attention. Exuding a wonderful presence, the book rotated several times, displaying alternately its front and back cover. Feeling that I was to be involved with the book somehow, I looked closely for the title, but to no avail.

Upon awakening, I immediately sensed someone walking away from my bedroom, and felt a thrilling, blissful voice say, "Bye." The voice was Nayaswami Anandi's; the dream and the blissful messenger were telling me that Anandi wanted this book made available to others. Within a week I discovered her manuscript, which had no title, in the hatch of our coffee table.

Anandi, circa 1975.

Anandi's focus in life was perfecting her discipleship to Master* and Swamiji. Once she had embarked on the spiritual path, she sought to make every moment one of service to her guru

_____

* Paramhansa Yogananda's disciples often address him lovingly as "Master."

and to Swamiji. In 1993, as Anandi described in the notes she left in the hatch, she had a dream that highlighted the choice every serious disciple must make:

> I stepped out of a car and immediately saw Swamiji, and said hello. Then I walked on but felt empty inside. I went back and replayed the dream. This time, as I got out of the car, I offered to cook for Swamiji. Then we began cooking together on the sidewalk.
>
> While helping Swamiji, I felt inside myself a joyous, intimate love—a love we want to feel all the time.

The important takeaway from the dream, Anandi goes on to explain, is something Swamiji once remarked: "I'm just here. People make of me what they will. Some people draw very close, others keep their distance inwardly, perhaps waiting to be invited."

Anandi continues, "Some people say, 'I'm willing to do whatever's needed!' With those, Swami works closely. The more we are willing to give, the closer drawn in we are.

"Once I felt Swami's energy more strongly, bliss, love, stillness began flowing to me—always flowing. Then I began praying to his energy and received a stronger response; and when I prayed to you [Master]—though I had never thought of your energy as being separate—praying to you acted as a password that allowed me to enter into your flow. I felt the veil lifting between you and me, and between Swami and me."

In her last correspondence with Swami Kriyananda, Anandi describes how his priceless gift of divine love thrills and transforms us:

> Dearest Swamiji,
>
> I write this message today, but the real message is written in my heart and mind every day as I think of you.
>
> Day by day, I am touched by awe, reverence, gratitude, and love for who you are, for what you give to the world, and for what you give to each of us.
>
> Your example of true, egoless discipleship and dedication to serving Master is a priceless gift that I draw from daily. The teachings expressed through your writings and talks increasingly fill me with wonder for their clarity and heart-touching depth.
>
> But what is most precious to me is your amazing love—a never-ending lesson in itself. Love that is so natural, humble, and filled with joy, humor, and understanding. Each of us feels uniquely loved by you.
>
> Swamiji, the last words you said to me were, "Thank you for your love through all these years." Thank *you* for bringing me back always to love.
>
> May I someday fulfill your priceless gifts by giving back to the world what you have given to me.

Paramhansa Yogananda
(1893-1952).

At another time, Anandi wrote these words to Yogananda:

> Thoughts of you fill my heart today. Two or three
> weeks ago I felt you looking thoughtfully at me and
> inwardly I heard you say, "The quirks have disap-
> peared." I think so too. When a ship is taken into
> pure water the barnacles drop off. Similarly, when
> God allows a devotee to live in the pure spiritual
> water that surrounds a guru, faults disappear with-
> out effort.

I have only one job. To keep my consciousness with You, to grow in love and joy and attunement. To keep my eye on the ball, in the present. To try to be connected to You in love and joy, and to share that through service at Ananda.

"The flow of our energy must be toward the spiritual eye—all the time." This principle Anandi sought always to follow. When she met with and counseled others, inwardly she would sense the energy at her spiritual eye and spine, then send Master's healing energy to whoever was in front of her. Many guests at Ananda Village have related that they felt Anandi truly *saw* them.

She loved helping others progress on the spiritual path, and was quite forthcoming about her own miscues when these could offer clarity and hope to others. Anandi never spoke, however, of her most sacred experiences. *Trained in Divine Love* shares many of these, precious experiences she has let me know she wishes to be shared. In deciding what to include, I have chosen those parts of Anandi's personal correspondence with Paramhansa Yogananda that are most instructive and deeply inspiring.

Part One of this book contains Anandi's stories of Swami Kriyananda, especially of how he helped her perfect her divine love and attunement. Part Two features excerpts from her personal correspondence with Master. Anandi wrote Yogananda each year on his birthday (January 5) and during her yearly seclusion. These excerpts capture the intimate dialogue that develops between devoted disciple and guru—even when the guru is no longer in the physical body.

Part Three includes "What Goes, What Stays," Nayaswami Jyotish's blog about Anandi's eternal qualities, and "Expanding Love": my account of Anandi's remarkable passage to higher realms, and how she continues to visit and bless devotees on earth.

✸ ✸ ✸ ✸ ✸

Anandi's sudden illness prevented her from finalizing her manuscript. It is my great honor to help Anandi (even in humble ways) bring forth her liberating message of total discipleship, and its glorious fruit: divine love. *Trained in Divine Love* is Anandi's gift to the Divine in all of us: that we immerse ourselves completely in God's perfect love and bliss.

Boundless blessings,
Nayaswami Bharat

Swami Kriyananda.

PART ONE

*My Life with
Swami Kriyananda*

The Early Years and Monasticism

I WAS CATAPULTED ONTO the spiritual path the morning of my twenty-third birthday. The night before, I'd gone to sleep, comfortable in my materialistic outlook—working, preparing for graduate school, making new friends my first year in Berkeley. The next morning I awoke literally desperate to touch a deeper part of myself, to touch the deeper meaning of life. The momentum of my desperation led me on a journey that ended with my arrival at Ananda Village the day before my twenty-fourth birthday. I knew almost nothing about the spiritual path beyond a year's practice of Transcendental Meditation. I had never heard of Paramhansa Yogananda or Indian teachings.

A friend I met in Canada mentioned he had a college friend who'd moved to a community called Ananda. The college friend, Shivani, had sent him a postcard from Ananda that said, "I'm so close now, I can almost touch it." The words resonated with me so deeply that I thought, "I must meet this woman. She may have the answers I need." Hearing of her postcard led me to hitchhike immediately from British Columbia to Ananda Village.

I was able to visit for only four days at that point, but those four days turned my life around. Experiencing Ananda and a little bit of yoga made me feel as if I'd crawled out from under a heavy rock into clear, warm sunshine.

I took the yoga and meditation I learned at Ananda with me, and practiced daily for several months. Special blessings that came into my life during that period made me feel ready to move to Ananda in April of 1971. I won't tarry to describe them, for my goal is to write about Swami Kriyananda.

The first time I greeted Swami Kriyananda, after moving to Ananda, he reached out and gave me a big hug. He did the same thing often thereafter. I think he saw how "new" I was and that I could use encouragement. Since then, I've actually felt that I had perhaps been with him on Master's path previously but had wandered away from it.

On my first day at Ananda, I had met the woman who had written the postcard. Though at the time I had never thought about reincarnation, it was obvious that Shivani and I had a connection from the past.

When I moved to Ananda in 1971, Shivani and two other women had a business making health food candy. I joined them. We worked in the garden in the mornings and made our healthy candy in the afternoons.

We barely broke even and rarely paid ourselves much of a salary—I remember one particularly successful month when we each earned ninety dollars. There were quite a few other small businesses at Ananda—some actually paid a tiny salary, others lost more than they made. I remember Swamiji telling the community that eventually our work at Ananda would be teaching, sharing Yogananda's message with all. At the time, the idea was incomprehensible to me.

During those first months, I saw Swamiji primarily at the Saturday classes he gave regularly or the Sunday service he gave every week. In addition to work, I practiced meditating and doing yoga postures, and studied the few books available to us: *Autobiography of a Yogi* and the *14 Steps* (now called *The Art and Science of Raja Yoga*). We also studied the Self-Realization Fellowship mail-order lessons, as Swami had encouraged us to do.

Early years at Ananda. Left to right: Swamiji, Devi, Anandi, and far right, Jyotish.

Four months after my arrival, Swamiji started the Friends of God monastery, and held an initial meeting for those interested. There were many dedicated young single people at Ananda at that time; Swami felt the monastery would help focus us on the path. I found this idea staggering. Having just arrived, I felt a monastic life was too scary a step for me. I actually left Ananda the weekend of that first meeting; afterwards I heard that Swamiji had asked where I was.

Though I tried to push the idea of monasticism away, it remained a big question in my mind.

December 1971 brought my first all-day Christmas meditation. To keep us all alert, Swamiji always opened the windows wide to the fresh, very cold outside air. While he seemed relaxed in a simple sweater and perhaps a lightweight woolen shawl, we were really cold, wrapped in blankets. The meditation was a challenge, but as it came to an end, we were left with a feeling of divine joy. The most memorable part of the experience was a tangible feeling of peace of mind and heart—a peace I continued to feel all through January.

The day after the all-day meditation, we had a Christmas party. On Christmas Day, we listened to Handel's *Messiah* and had a banquet. Swamiji took these traditions from Master's Christmases in Los Angeles and recreated them for us.

Relatively early in my stay at Ananda, Swamiji went on a trip, I think to India. He sent a message to us on cassette, and many of us gathered in one of the businesses to listen. He sent a group message for all of us, and private messages for a number of people, including one for me: "Develop devotion!" And one more sentence after that, I think, "The minutes are more important than the years." I was embarrassed for everyone to hear that I needed devotion—as if they couldn't tell. But it was wonderful that he knew who I was and exactly what I needed!

In the spring of 1972, instead of joining the monastery, I had a little cabin built for me at the Meditation Retreat. The builder was an unfortunate person, full of negativity and doubt. I thought that I could surely help him, but after a couple of months of working together, I was a confused mess, filled with doubts and misery. I got a ride to Swamiji's dome and asked him what I should do. He commented: "You have too much ego. Ego attracts ego."

He then asked if the man had to finish the house. When I said I thought it would be awkward to stop the process at this point, he said simply: "Go into silence." I did so immediately, and found that my consciousness changed right away (Swamiji's loving thoughts were probably a key).

I lived in that little cabin at the Meditation Retreat through the winter, and kept our health food candy business going. The question always revolving in my mind:

Should I join the monastery? I feared that at twenty-five and so new on the path, I didn't have the wisdom to make such a significant life commitment. Others of my friends joined, but I just didn't feel enough clarity to do so.

During the winter, I had to go to St. Louis to take care of my dad while my mom was traveling. Because I was away from Ananda, I had a chance to stand back and ask, "Who am I? What is important to me?" At a certain point a letter arrived from Shivani: Two of the monastics, two people I looked to as sterling examples of renunciation, had decided to marry. I knew they would continue to be great renunciates always.

I remember the moment I read those words. I felt (as Gyanamata once wrote) that a window had opened in my mind and a cool breeze blown through. My overanxious thoughts about lifelong commitment and the pressure those thoughts placed on me were relieved. I felt the freedom to say to God: I choose YOU. If I am meant to marry, I put it entirely in Your hands.

When I returned to Ananda, I made an appointment with Swamiji to tell him that I wanted to join the monastery. I remember him looking at me with so much joy in his eyes, happy that I had made a good decision. He blessed me. I said: "Do I need to know anything?" He said: "No, you already know what you need to know." And that was the truth. Once I had embraced the idea of monasticism, it was as if lifetimes of what that meant came back to me: living for God.

Swami Kriyananda center, Anandi next right, circa 1973.

In 1973 I left the Meditation Retreat to move to the monastery. One of the monks had found a decrepit shell of a trailer for three-hundred dollars and moved it to the women's area for me. With lots of elbow grease and the help of a friend who could do some carpentry, I created what was for me a simple dream home. The tin lizzie wood stove was insulated from the walls only by aluminum foil. Often at night, I'd wake up to find the stove glowing red hot. I think only God's grace kept the trailer from catching fire and burning down.

A highlight of my years at the monastery was Christmas morning breakfasts for the nuns and monks at Swamiji's dome. The nuns would fix the breakfast.

One Christmas morning I felt tired and moody as I walked to Swamiji's for our breakfast. As each person ahead of me got to the door, Swamiji greeted him the same way: "Happy Christmas, Seva. Happy Christmas, Asha," and so on. When I got to the door, he changed his greeting, and said with great joy and love, "How is your Christmas, Anandi?" Faced with his beautiful energy, there was only one answer possible: "Wonderful, Swamiji!" And in saying that, the cloud lifted from my consciousness, and I had a wonderful Christmas.

Swamiji purposely created the vibration of being our friend. He said, "I've always felt I could help people best in the role of friend." Many spiritual teachers seem to enjoy the role of teacher or guru. Though Swami certainly had the right to embrace such a role, he did the exact opposite. He was always natural with us, making sure everyone felt comfortable to laugh and joke with him. He never projected an aura that would encourage us to put him on a pedestal.

I fully accepted his definition of himself, his way of seeing his role. Though I had experienced miracles that had come into my life through Swami, though I had clearly experienced him reading my mind, or using spiritual power from a distance, I still maintained a sense of relative ease around him. Though his greatness was revealed to me numerous times, I never fully realized who he was; I feel he successfully created a veil to help us be natural—both with him and with one another.

One weekend afternoon, as I was sitting in my trailer, I heard someone call, "Anandi." The voice was exquisite, and spoke my name so beautifully—like a magical being calling my soul, affirming my soul nature. It turned out to be Swamiji looking for Seva or Asha. But hearing his voice without knowing who was speaking was memorable. The feeling is still with me.

One time, during those early years, Swamiji wanted to take Prita and her boyfriend on a trip to LA to see Disneyland. He invited Parvati and me to go along. Our outing came during the time many members were attending the Self-Realization Fellowship convocation. Swami was then encouraging us to take the SRF lessons and be part of SRF.* One of the SRF monastics had called the Ananda participants at the convocation into a private room and then spoken very strongly against Swamiji. Swami used our trip south (probably based on his intuition of just what did happen) to take everyone to Disneyland and spend quite a bit of time talking to those who'd been at the convocation.

The story of his relationship with SRF emerged only gradually over the years.

In the early days of the monastery, the monks and nuns were friendly toward each other. For a time, I taught a

* Paramhansa Yogananda founded Self-Realization Fellowship in 1920. In 1950, he put twenty-three-year-old Kriyananda in charge of his male monastics. In 1960, Swami Kriyananda was elected to the SRF Board of Directors and also as SRF's first vice-president.

high school class with one of the monks, Ram Tirtha, and we were pals.

One night, Swamiji called the monastics together to share what Master had told his monks and nuns: "After I'm gone, if ever I find you fraternizing, I'll come back from wherever I am and blow this organization out of existence." Swamiji told us not to look into the eyes of someone of the opposite sex, nor to mix in a social way. We were all galvanized by his words. As we left the satsang we were bumping into one another, because we were looking only at the floor, lest we meet someone's eyes.

After that meeting, I let Ram Tirtha take over the class.

When I joined the monastery, I remember feeling that I had joined monasteries in the past. Perhaps as a holdover from those earlier incarnations, for quite a while whenever I went into my meditation room, I'd feel, "You aren't sincere. If you were, you'd meditate much more." The feeling seemed right to me, and was quite depressing.

After struggling for a month or so, I made an appointment to see Swamiji. While explaining what was happening to me, I couldn't help but shed a few tears. Swamiji's response was unexpected and sudden: He whacked me on top of my head, and said, "Mosquito." My energy shot up my spine; I'd needed that!

Swamiji's description of my paralyzing mood: "It's Satan."

During those early years, we often had swamis come to visit Ananda. Most of them were beautiful and quite respectful of our Swamiji. One swami came while Swamiji was away—possibly in India in 1973? Many were attracted to him and three ended up leaving Ananda to follow him. He didn't interest me much, though Shivani was drawn to him. He made great claims for his spirituality. He said: "If Swamiji knew who I am, he would turn the community over to me." On his return, Swamiji was not pleased to hear of this, and not impressed with those words. "Who is he?" he asked. "Even if he were Lahiri Mahasaya, I've created this community for Master." After that fiasco, we mostly stopped having visiting swamis.

Swami Venkateshananda (disciple of Sivananda) came sometime after that while Swamiji was in residence. He seemed to be one of the greatest we'd met. Highly respectful of Swamiji, he said: "As long as Swami is alive, you'll never know who he really is." He meant that Swamiji was hiding his greatness from us.

In 1974 I started working for Ananda Publications (now called Crystal Clarity Publishers) to promote Swamiji's books. Swamiji had heard Master's strong statements about upcoming disasters and felt duty-bound to share those predictions, which he incorporated into a small book called *The Road Ahead*. Swamiji began to craft possible ads for the books: large flames, people standing in breadlines—quite intense images. Despite being only

Anandi working at Ananda Publications, 1974.

twenty-seven and having no previous experience, I dis-agreed with his approach.

I remember a drive to the Meditation Retreat for Sunday service when Swamiji took me to task for criticizing his ideas. I didn't understand why he was severe and tried to figure it out inside myself. I came to the conclusion that he didn't like negativity; he wanted to hear positive alternatives. The real reason, of course, was that how he presented Master's teachings was his business, that I was his extremely inexperienced employee and student, and that I should try to get with the program. But I wasn't yet capable of this level of understanding.

What I did was to come up with some positive alternative ads and take them to his dome to show him. He gave me no energy for these great ideas. I was still not getting it. The next day, Asha and I had to drive together to the San Francisco Bay Area. At a certain point, she calmly said, "Swamiji didn't like your ideas." I am embarrassed to say, but it must be admitted, I replied, "Well, he's an author, and he has a certain ego about his ideas." Her calm response—God bless you, Asha!—was: "Who do you think has more ego, Swamiji or you?" Her words were a radical departure from my usual way of thinking—though in retrospect painfully obvious. At the time, hearing her words, I felt I was being shot upwards in a rocket to a new level of clarity. Wow. How grateful I was for this experience! Swamiji had told her she needed to help me, and she did. Though I still had a lot to learn subsequently, that moment brought a key lesson.

In the late 1970s Swami asked two members to create a slide show, using his slides, music, and written script. They worked on it for a couple of months and created something nice. But Swamiji felt it needed improvement in order to be shown at our Spiritual Renewal Week that year at the Meditation Retreat. He asked Asha and me to help him.

During early Spiritual Renewal Weeks, Swami taught all the morning classes, often counseled guests in the afternoon, and also gave the evening programs. After his Monday morning class that year, Asha and I went with him into Nevada City to David Praver's home—David had not yet moved to Ananda Village—where we would have consistent electricity—electricity at the Ananda Retreat,

which ran on generators, was anything but consistent—
and plenty of room to work.

Going through the current slide show in David's base-
ment, we realized that what we needed to do was not a
simple project. We had to synchronize music, slides, and
words. The slide show had to be recreated from the beginning. I think Swami had hoped to finish in the afternoon.
When he realized how much work was involved, I could
feel him ratchet up his energy. He didn't say anything;
he simply went into a higher gear—not nervously, not
tensely, simply increasing the concentration and energy
flowing through him.

The script needed extensive editing. Once he'd finished, he
handed the edited version to me to take upstairs to type.
I've never been a fast typist, and I usually make mistakes
when I type. But the flow of energy through Swamiji was
also lifting Asha and me up. I began to type faster than I
ever had, but most surprisingly to me, with NO mistakes.
I felt that the energy was using me. I was not the doer. At
a certain point Swami left us, either to do the evening program or to get some sleep before his morning class. Asha
and I worked through the night. The next morning before
class, we happily presented the finished project to Swami.

When people sympathized with us because we hadn't
slept, Swamiji commented that the sympathy was
misplaced, that it was a blessing to be able to serve as we
had. We certainly agreed with him.

Anandi meditating in The Meditation Retreat Temple, Ananda Village, 1980.

A funny memory: One Saturday morning, Swamiji was giving a Meditation Retreat class on Spiritual Astrology. I was sitting on my kneeling bench immediately in front of him. The talk was a bit technical for me, and the day was warm; soon I was swaying and nodding off. Suddenly, in a loud voice, Swami said: "Anandi, you're an Aries aren't you?" Wow! I was suddenly wide awake!

Swamiji was an open channel for Master to speak to us. He kept his mind connected to his guru; when an inspiration to say something came, he said it. One Sunday after the service, Swamiji had lunch with Seva, Asha, and me; because Swamiji and I sat facing Seva and Asha, he and I were looking in the same direction. Sometime earlier, Swamiji had begun receiving letters from a very sincere devotee I'll call N. I was aware of this man's interest in Master and Ananda but was not very involved in his exchange with Swamiji. Then N arrived at Ananda. Uh-oh. He was cute. Though I hadn't spoken to him, I began to feel an at-traction to him. God made sure it was short-lived! As we all sat together, N went through the lunch line in front of Swamiji and me. Swamiji said, as if disparagingly, "Look at that man! He looks as if life has really beaten him down!" In that moment, I felt inwardly a joyous release from my attraction. It was over in that instant, replaced by happiness and knowing that Master and Swamiji were taking care of me. Meanwhile, Seva and Asha were quite confused—they knew how highly Swamiji thought of this disciple and couldn't imagine why he would criticize him. In time, we all came to realize that when Swamiji said something unusual like that, it was for the benefit of someone in the room.

In 1974, when Ananda acquired the land adjacent to the Farm area, the Nevada County Planning Department took notice of us. They realized that Ananda Village was much more than its original designation as a "Church Camp"—that we needed to file a Master Plan for our property. Our neighbor Sam Dardick, a professional planner, offered his services to Ananda. Working in my office in the Publications Building, I heard Swamiji talking with a group in a nearby room: "I want Anandi to do it." Afterwards, I asked him what he wanted me to do. He explained that Sam wanted a secretary-writer for the Master Plan, and that he thought I could fill that role. In surprise, I asked him, "Did you know that I had started graduate school to study city planning?" No, he hadn't—but, once again, God had flowed through him. I had attended graduate school for only ten weeks before I dropped out to move to Ananda. But the interest and the karma were there, and God flowed through him to offer me the opportunity.

When Swamiji was working on his autobiography, *The Path* (now revised as *The New Path*), he asked another woman to create an index for the book. I felt very attracted to that job. When the woman decided to leave Ananda, I prayed for guidance, and then wrote Swamiji that I would love to do the index. His instructions were to put into the index the name of every person he included in the book. Also, he wanted every story about Master to be indexed by the quality it expressed. What a marvelous job that was! I did the indexing on notecards—we didn't have computers in 1975—and needed to go over the book many times to check my work. Sometimes when I was sitting hunched over my desk working, Swamiji would come in and whack me behind the heart. Probably he wanted me to sit up straighter (in Master's words, "a bent spine is the enemy of Self-realization"), but I imagine he was also helping open my heart center and awaken my intuition.

During Swami's seclusion in India in 1976 and 1977, I discovered Frank Laubach's book, *Letters of a Modern Mystic*, and was thrilled by it. I read it often and carried it around with me. I mailed a copy to Swamiji in India. He responded, "I was just wishing I could have a copy of that book."

He had met Frank Laubach years before and considered him a saint.

After he returned from India, during the next two years (1978-79), he set off with a dozen or so singers and staff on Ananda's Joy Tours, lecturing in large cities across the United States. At one point, detouring from a visit to my parents in St. Louis, I flew to join the tour for a week or so. In New York, he told a story he often used to tell about a timid little girl who had to be in a school performance. When she came on stage she froze. Someone in the audience called out, "Don't worry, Suzy, we're all on your side." He would tell the story to remind us that God is on our side. This time, in New York, in telling the story, he said, "Don't worry, Margie, we're all on your side." Margie is my birth name. As Swamiji told the story, I felt him reaching out to me to help me overcome my own lack of self-confidence.

At a satsang in Swami's dome, I think in the early 1980s, we were, as usual, squashing in. I often tried to sit as near him as possible. I had positioned myself right in front of him with a couple of feet between us. As people crowded in, we in front kept moving closer and closer to Swamiji till I was practically touching him. He led us in a prayer and a chant and then into a short meditation before his talk.

As he began that meditation, he was absolutely still. I believe he was breathless. The stillness around him was so profound that I myself couldn't breathe—not, unfortunately, from my own absorption, but because I was overwhelmed by his breathless state. Because I realized what was happening, my experience of shortness of breath, though not pleasant, became deeply inspiring.

A Renunciate Marriage

A T A CERTAIN POINT I began to feel that the monastery, where I'd fully expected to spend my life, wasn't fitting me anymore. The feeling of not fitting was at first vague. Then—I won't go into the story—I sensed that Master wanted me to marry Bharat. I went to see Swamiji. Swami's advice: "Meditate and ask Master what you should do." Time passed and Bharat and I drew closer together. I wrote Swami how I was feeling. Some time later, when I saw him in the Temple foyer, I told him that Bharat and I seemed to be moving toward a commitment. What did he think? Swami's reply: "I think it would be good for you."

More than a year later, as the date for our marriage approached, I began to get cold feet. I'd never been able to commit to a relationship. Now I began to wonder if Bharat was really the right person for me. I wrote my doubts to Swamiji. He had Seva write his reply. She wrote, "Swamiji says your concerns are because you're thinking too much of yourself. Think of Bharat and how you can help him." Yes! That spoke to me perfectly, and has turned out to be a guiding star in my married life.

In 1983, Swamiji performed Anandi and Bharat's wedding.

Bharat and I were married in a ceremony with two other couples; of the six of us, four had been in the monastery. Swamiji spoke of the significance of so many monastics entering married life—that Ananda was moving toward all of life being renunciation.

The years brought me many challenges in how I related to Swamiji. I had difficulty understanding who he was—understanding the unconditional love he was offering each of us. The year Swamiji's mother died, Bharat, Keshava, and I were running the Cooperative Spiritual Living program at the house on Tyler Foote Road. Swamiji gave a very touching service for his mother. For reasons I cannot fathom, the service brought up emotion in me; I felt left out. I wrote him an emotional letter. Afterward, when I saw him at Crystal Hermitage, he very calmly said, "What happened?" I appreciated his calm words; they showed me that he knew I would work myself through the emotion and come out the other side—that our true connection was on a deeper level, deeper than and unaffected by the alien emotional turmoil that would from time to time pop up and need to be dealt with.

Outside the early version of Swamiji's dome—before it was completely remodeled—he installed a large plastic swimming pool and often had pool parties. At one of these parties, the women were doing water ballet at one end of the pool, and at the other end the men began playing Horse. I sat between the two and enjoyed the contrast. For the game of Horse, I think it was Danny who had Swamiji on his shoulders, Dr. Peter who was the "horse" for the challenger. One man after another would climb on Dr. Peter's shoulders and try to unseat Swamiji. It was quite playful, and Swamiji easily unseated all of them. I remember someone I thought of as close to Swami (he's no longer at Ananda) who fell into the water at the very first touch Swamiji gave him.

Not so with Bharat. I watched with something like horror as Bharat climbed aboard to challenge Swamiji. The intensity in his face and body showed that he fully intended to unseat Swamiji. I was alarmed at what I considered an inappropriate attitude. I needn't have worried. In moments Bharat was in the water like those before him. The next day at Sunday service, Swamiji praised Bharat's approach: If you're going to do something, give it all you've got. Gracious as always, Swamiji didn't mention who won the challenge.

Atherton House

IN 1983 (a few months after our wedding) Swamiji asked us, together with Parvati, to move to Atherton to run the Ananda center there. Sometimes he would visit us.

One Sunday afternoon, after we'd been there awhile, I found myself going through a dry period. Swamiji was visiting San Francisco and giving a little satsang at the San Francisco ashram. Though I hated to have Swami see me like this, I knew I needed to be around him. Bharat and I came into the gathering in the ashram a few minutes late.

A small group were sitting in a circle talking about Swami's new album of music based on the life of St. Francis. One song is called "Life Flows On like a River." When I first heard it, the song didn't appeal to me. No sooner had Bharat and I joined the circle than Swamiji said, "Anandi, what do you think of 'Life Flows On like a River'?" Yikes. Well, I said something like, "Swamiji, I'm not a very musical person and I can't explain it, but for some reason I just don't like that song."

His response was amazing. You would have thought I'd made a brilliant comment. With great interest and enthusiasm he responded as if to a famous music critic. His response was, on one level, a beautiful example of living perfectly the guideline to see praise and blame as equal. Later, as I walked with him down the hall, he turned to a person who'd come up and once again, with great delight, said, Anandi doesn't like "Life Flows On like a River"—as if I were a brilliant prodigy.

When I commented on this memory years later, Swamiji said that he was pleased that I had responded with a blend of kindness and honesty. But I think that, seeing my need for blessings, and having only my comment to work with, he gave me great support for my words. Even more recently, the insight came that in my honesty I stayed connected to Swamiji. If I'd tried to say nice words about the music in order to try to "please" him, I would have put a distance between us. It was much more pleasing to him that I was genuine, and thereby showed my trust in our bond of love—my freedom from any thought that I needed to flatter him.

The builders who lived in our Atherton house did a lot of work to remodel the little pool cabin into a nice space for Swamiji. I hadn't noticed that there were daddy longlegs spiders still on the ceiling. When Swamiji commented about them, I made a joke about the little cabin being a bit decrepit. Swamiji made it clear that the point wasn't the cabin's condition but the spiders—I needed to get the spiders out of there.

Shortly after the little cabin was ready, Swamiji brought his fiancée, Rosanna, her parents, and her aunt to stay with us. Swamiji and Rosanna stayed in the cabin, and we found nice accommodations elsewhere for her relatives; we hosted a number of meals for them at our house. Swamiji was pleased with the stay. As he was leaving, I walked him to the car, with him resting his left arm on my shoulder, and I resting my right hand on his back. For many months, an ugly wart on that right hand hadn't responded to any treatment. The day after walking Swamiji to the car, I noticed the wart was simply gone. The thought came to me: "Where God's light is, no darkness can dwell."

On a pilgrimage with Swamiji to Los Angeles, I felt so uplifted by his discipleship ceremony that I walked back to my room barefooted, and had to go back for my shoes. He phoned and invited us, along with about twenty others, to go out to a restaurant for dinner. Quite an elegant restaurant. Naively we kept ordering refills on the non-alcoholic wine. The bill came to something like seventy-five dollars per couple, an exceptional sum in those days. It was a special and lovely evening.

I think it was on that same pilgrimage that when I came forward for a blessing Swamiji said, "Live in the thought of God; you are God." Deeply important for me.

But when I found out he'd said to Bharat, "Master is very pleased with you," a murky emotion rose from the depths and I began crying—feeling that I wasn't as good as Bharat, wasn't worthy to receive that ultimate praise. The crying came not during the dinner, but the next day. Swami saw me weeping.

From the pilgrimage we returned to Atherton house; Swamiji was staying overnight. The next morning I had a very calm meditation. When I saw Swamiji later that morning, he said, "What was it?" I responded, "I'm sorry. It's fine now."

When Swamiji was buying wedding rings, he looked at ours and said, "That's nice, but I want something more joyful!" He applied himself to everything he did. Their wedding rings were a band of gold flowers with tiny diamonds in the center of each flower, very beautiful.

We went with Swamiji and Rosanna on a pilgrimage to Israel in 1986. We had flown in; they would be arriving later that night. The pilgrimage group included all of Swamiji's "in-crowd." That assessment was not his but mine (and, I think, the "in-crowd's"). To wait together for Swamiji's arrival for a number of hours, Bharat and I would need to impose ourselves on that group—all tight friends with one another. Unfortunately, Bharat and I went to sleep instead—a choice on my part based on feeling unwanted by that group (most of whom no longer live at Ananda). The next morning, we greeted Swamiji. He greeted us warmly and said, "Where were you?" I had made the wrong choice.

One of the places I most wanted to see on that pilgrimage was the Mount of Transfiguration. Riding in a speeding cab as it swerved its way up the mountain made me a bit ill; when we arrived and sat to meditate, I kept nodding off. Swamiji himself had been extremely ill when he arrived in Israel—the last stage of his and Rosanna's round-the-world honeymoon. As we left the chapel on the Mount, Swami said—I think for my benefit—"When I want God as much as I want sleep, I'll be free." On one hand, his words were comforting—I assumed he'd been as sleepy as I. But because sleep is so magnetic for me, his words were also a message for me, one that I reflect on often.

A married couple, part of our Palo Alto congregation, were supposed to be part of the Holy Land pilgrimage, but backed out at the last moment to go somewhere with Sant Keshavadas. When I told Swami they were following Sant Keshavadas instead, Swami commented, "He must have something I don't have." I said, "Yes, he does." Swami looked at me with a question in his eyes. I went on, "He flatters their egos." Swami responded, "Yes, but then what do you have?"

Ananda Meditation Retreat

ASHA AND DAVID PRAVER, now ready to move to the Peninsula, came and joined us for a few weeks in 1986. We were supposed to go back to the Village for a short vacation and then return. When we got to the Village, Swamiji said, "We're starting our training program for new members. Others have been suggested, but I said we need our strongest devotees for this. Would you do it?" Of course we said yes.

I think he knew that a partnership with Asha and David wouldn't work well for any of us. They really didn't need us down there. Swamiji's comment about why he had sent us to Palo Alto in the first place was, "It's hard to find people willing to take responsibility." I think we were placeholders until the Pravers were ready to come. His instructions to us about going there had been, "Be people's friends." His instructions to Asha and David

Satsang for new Ananda members with Rosanna Walters, second row fourth from the right. Bharat and Anandi, first row, first and second from the right. Crystal Hermitage, 1989.

were, "There are six million people in the Bay Area to bring to these teachings." He felt they had what it took to really build the work there.

We were happy to move to the Meditation Retreat and start the program. It was designed initially as a three-month training, then became a two-month training, followed by a year of living at the Retreat in its small community.

Swamiji sometimes stayed in his dome at the Meditation Retreat, and when his marriage with Rosanna broke up, he lived at the Retreat full time. When the Temple collapsed, Swami gave us his dome to use as a temporary temple, and he moved back to Crystal Hermitage. Still, during our eight years at the Meditation Retreat we had a number of lovely experiences with Swamiji. The events described below are not in chronological order.

A woman named Elizabeth (who later received from Swamiji the name Lahari) had a special relationship with Swamiji. One day, Swami said to me, "Elizabeth and her husband are coming by on Saturday. Would you fix lunch for us?" With a lot of joy, I prepared the meal, which Bharat and I happily delivered to serve the three of them. Elizabeth and her husband were gone. Swami said, "Oh, they were here just for a short time; this is for us." It was a special joy, because I'd felt only happiness in making the lunch for others—with no sense of being left out. I felt I'd gotten the lesson.

A Time of Testing

OUR TIME AT the Meditation Retreat was not always easy. I was ill in ways that drained my energy. Bharat became ill in the early 1990s with sarcoidosis, a rare and debilitating disease that causes inflammation throughout the body—in Bharat, manifesting especially in tumors in the lymph system surrounding his heart. For three years, he suffered from severe weakness and almost daily bouts of fever. Finally, the symptoms abated and his strength began to return. But because his lungs had been affected, he coughed continually, sometimes for five minutes at a time.

Swamiji, himself recovering from open-heart surgery, asked Bharat and me to come over briefly to discuss a certain matter. Although sarcoidosis is not contagious, on the way to the Hermitage I said to Bharat, "Perhaps you shouldn't expose Swamiji to your cough. You could wait upstairs while I go down to his apartment to see him." Bharat agreed.

When Swamiji sent word that he wanted both of us to come down, Bharat went too, but he stood a little away from Swamiji and let me do the talking.

As we were about to leave, I explained, "Bharat has been coughing for six months."

Swamiji looked at Bharat, and in a strong but matter-of-fact way said, "Bharat doesn't have a cough."

At that moment, the cough stopped and never returned. Swamiji's blessing lifted Bharat over the last karmic hurdle of that long illness.

During the years of Bharat's illness, there was no cure or relief. We were both under a lot of pressure and pretty isolated at the Meditation Retreat. One day, I prayed deeply to Swamiji. That same evening, I went to Ananda's Expanding Light Retreat for an event. Swamiji's secretary came up to me and said, "Please come to Crystal Hermitage tomorrow. Swamiji has a project for you." He wanted me to write the subheadings for *Awaken to Superconsciousness*. Clearly, a job created in response to my prayer.

On another occasion, in response to my prayer to Swamiji when I was again feeling isolated, the very next day at a meeting at his home, he gave me a project to work on: connecting the affirmations we read at our Sunday services with the readings in his book, *Rays of the One Light*. Both times, I was deeply touched that he'd received my prayer and answered it.

At a point in my stay at the Meditation Retreat when his secretary had to be away, Swamiji asked me to fill in. Happy as I was to serve in this way, I found the job challenging—frustrating computer problems and not much of an IT department to ask for help.

One day during my time at Crystal Hermitage, Swamiji called us down to his apartment to tell us he was feeling very ill, and wouldn't be working with us. The feeling in his apartment, however, was not of his illness but of over-whelming bliss.

During Swamiji's editing of *The Rubaiyat of Omar Khayyam Explained*, he asked me to read an editorial comment. I had to tell him that what he'd written didn't make any sense. He said, "I was afraid you'd say that." That evening, I got a phone call at the Meditation Retreat. Swamiji said, "I've rewritten that comment; please listen with concentration." The new version is actually one of the highlights of the book. (Look it up, it's stanza 31.)

Anandi and Swami Kriyananda at his 1986 birthday party, Crystal Hermitage.

On another day, I was sitting in our living room at the Retreat. Bharat had gone on a nature adventure and was late coming home. I didn't feel concern, for I felt the loving presence of God very beautifully and strongly. The phone rang and it was Swamiji—he shared with me a wonderfully blissful and loving vibration. He was reaching out to me. Another time I was sitting in the Expanding Light Temple as Nayaswami Gyandev began his class with a short meditation. The feeling of my meditation was especially beautiful and God-filled—I felt myself soaring. Someone came into the room to get me: "Swamiji's on the phone for you." Both times Swamiji called to affirm our loving connection. I believe he sent the love in front of his calls. During both phone calls, there was a marvelous flow of love between us.

On Thanksgiving, about 1997, though I was very tired, I attended the evening's music and stories by Tim and Jeannie because I heard Swamiji would be there. He sat in the front row, deeply absorbed in meditation. Suddenly my whole chest/heart opened like a huge cavern filled with love and joy. I have never experienced anything like it. I thought I must be feeling what Swamiji was feeling.

The Expanding Light and Other Reminiscences

WHEN SWAMIJI MOVED to Italy in about 1998, we flew over to attend a weeklong course that he gave. We went to every event, but never saw Swamiji privately; I felt badly not to spend personal time with him. On our last day there, however, I felt so uplifted at his satsang that I completely forgot my earlier sadness. I walked Swami to his car and told him we were leaving the next day. He said, "Oh, then you should come to tea with us in Assisi."

During the tea, I told Swami that something he'd said that morning had hit me like cold water thrown on me. Just at this point in my story, I inadvertently knocked over my glass of water so that it shattered on the floor. Swamiji made a comment about Margie Stern (my birth name). I realized he was saying I needed to be more centered than I was presently being—not to be acting like my old self as "Margie Stern." The juxtaposition of my remark with the accident had struck me as funny, but Swami saw the true lesson behind the surface humor.

When Swamiji was in the body, many of us had a natural wish to spend time with him privately. Most of those Swami felt comfortable having around him frequently were the ones he was training to take over Ananda in the future; he wanted every opportunity to infuse them with his vibrations. Others were never invited to those smaller gatherings, either because they didn't have such a role, or because they didn't have that karma with him. And quite a few others, including Bharat and me, were sometimes invited and sometimes not.

Being around Swamiji was like nothing else in my experience. The level of inspiration, love, and joy was marvelous. He saw the highest in everyone; in his presence that best part in you came out. Over time those blessings were transformative. Even *not* being around Swamiji brought its own blessings—the opportunity to get over those high school in-group/out-group feelings.

In, I think, 1974, when I was working on the Master Plan, Swamiji took Seva, Asha, Keshava, and me to town for a hearing. On the way back, he asked questions about the plan that I answered. In the middle of what I thought was a good discussion Swami suddenly stopped at Ayodhya under the big oak tree. Graciously he asked if I would like to get out near my trailer. In the next breath, he asked the others if they would like to come to tea. Exquisite pain. I remember sitting in my trailer, understanding perfectly why he had acted as he had. I needed to get beyond that in-group/out-group energy—to reconnect with my purpose in being at Ananda. It was the same test I've had to work with over the years. This and other experiences of testing probably proved more important to me in the long run than being invited to join the tea. Swamiji always used his time wisely to help us in the best way—with encouragement, with tests, with whatever was most useful.

Writing down many of these incidents is painful, because they so often reveal my spiritual denseness, my lack of understanding of how to treat the blessing of a personal teacher and messenger sent to me by God and Guru, and above all my self-involvement or emotional imbalances. This morning, however, I realize the blessing of the painful self-awareness brought by each test. Swamiji came to reveal everything to me—not only the vision of liberation, the steps on the path, the right attitudes, but also to bring clearly to mind what *I* needed to work on. Though in the moment I stumbled, I often—even if usually later (perhaps moments, weeks, or decades later)—grasped what the right attitude should have been. I hope that in flushing out some of these wrong attitudes into my awareness, they are also flushed from my consciousness!

The most important thing for me to remember—what I have been feeling much more clearly since Swamiji's passing—is the depth of who he is, the profound love he has for each of us, and the blessings from him that are available to us every moment.

Several instances of the intuitive flow between us occurred to me as I awoke this morning. Last night I went to bed a bit discouraged by memory after memory of missing the point. No matter how often the little, selfish ego tripped, Swamiji was always my polestar of how to be, how to behave, how to love God and people. The essential lesson for the devotee is to look always toward one's aspirations, never to identify with temporary flashes of ignorance.

The stories that came to me as I awoke were, I think, sent by Swamiji or Master to get me back on track.

Starting in 1984 or '85 I had sharp pains in my left foot and calf. Because of their location, they were easy to ignore; I saw them as karma burning off and wasn't concerned. But when a chiropractor discovered a lump in my left calf, I went to St. Louis to get it checked out with a CT scan and MRI. At that time at Ananda I hadn't yet watched so many saintly friends handle cancer; not knowing what to expect, I was getting nervous. When I phoned Swamiji from St. Louis, he said simply, "I will pray for you." Instantly I felt completely calm, able to take each day as it came. This calmness lasted for quite a while, and was accompanied by the small miracle of the surgeon not charging us for his services.

The lump turned out to be a neuroma—not cancerous. In 1990, a similar lump appeared in my left wrist, again quite painful but easily ignored. On a trip to the nearby Sierra Family Medical Clinic, I drew one of Master's Para-grams, which at that time were given out to patients. My Para-gram's theme was willpower. Willpower was what I needed to put out to deal with the pain in my wrist. In 1991, after our pilgrimage to India, I contacted the hand surgeon who had been on the pilgrimage with us. I was confident about the process this time, but asked Swamiji for prayers. Because Durga was having major surgery at the time, I didn't mention mine to anyone but Swamiji.

The day after surgery in Palo Alto, I awoke in a blissful state, one of the most blissful I've ever experienced—one of the spiritual highlights of my life. A group of us went for a walk. As we walked by a house in Mountain View, I said, "Listen: chanting!" When the others listened, they said, "What are you talking about? That's reggae music." I heard only devotional music. I can only assume that the source was Swami's blessing. This time too, because he was part of Ananda, the surgeon didn't charge me for his services.

In 1986, at a time when we were once again confronted by problems with Self-Realization Fellowship, Bharat and I came up to the Village from the Atherton Ashram for a class of Swami's the next day. In the morning I couldn't meditate. I kept thinking of Daya Mata and what we could do to demonstrate to her who Swamiji really was. That morning at The Expanding Light, we waited a long time for Swamiji to appear for his class. When he finally arrived, he said that he was late because he had received a phone call from Daya Mata that morning. I had attuned to the vibration of the phone call.

When, by 1991, the lawsuit was threatening, I kept feeling to write to SRF to tell them who we were at Ananda and what our life here was like. When I phoned Devi to share my thought, she responded that Swamiji had already decided who was to contact SRF. I let the idea go. Later, Devi told me that Swamiji did want me to write a letter to SRF. She also told me that when Swami heard I'd already been feeling to write SRF, he commented, "Anandi must be in tune." I went to his office, and he asked me my thoughts. Though I felt I had little to share, I did write the letter; Swami contacted me to say he liked what I had written.

I've been reflecting on how Swamiji was always LISTENING. What did this look like? No matter what he was doing, he was inwardly still. Even practicing the Energization Exercises—with their many movements— you could feel his deep stillness. Swamiji gave thousands of lectures, each one involving a great deal of speaking. Yet, as he often pointed out, he was always listening to the audience—what did they need to hear?

I saw Swami speak from inner listening directly in my own life and indirectly in accounts related by others. Sometimes when Swamiji was speaking to a small or large group of people, he would say something seemingly unrelated, or even strange. Yet there would be one person in the audience for whom it was a particularly enlightening comment.

In, I think, 1987, I went through a strange phase: Whatever comment I made to Swamiji, he would reply as if I'd said something else. Feeling quite confused, I began to harbor the thought, "He doesn't understand me." After as much as a year of this miscommunication, there came a turning point. I was sitting right in front of him at a satsang in the Hermitage living room. A fellow devotee said something and I commented on the statement. My comment seemed to me extremely clear, yet once again Swami responded as if I'd said something very different.

At that point conversation stopped. Swamiji stopped speaking and looked at me while I went inside my head, and once again, thought, "He doesn't understand me!" Following close on that thought was another: "That's a ridiculous idea to hold on to. Of course he understands me." As soon as I completed that second thought, as if Swami had been waiting for me to release that delusion, conversation resumed.

That evening, since Swami was staying at the Meditation Retreat (where Bharat and I lived at the time), we visited him in his dome. All I can say about my conversation with Swamiji is that there was an intuitive flow: As I thought something, he would respond to that very thought. We went back and forth in perfect harmony for a few minutes. It seemed to be his way of showing me what was really going on between us. He understood me quite well, was listening to my thought processes, and (I assume) all along had been helping me release some old karma of mine.

Swamiji said that he held all of us in his aura. Several times I experienced being so held. One summer evening, while we were living at the Meditation Retreat, from the kitchen where I was cooking dinner I could hear nearby the sound of a borate bomber. Not seeing any signs of fire, I wasn't concerned. Then the phone rang. Swamiji was calling for me—he wanted to let me know that I had made a mistake in how I had handled something. I don't think he had ever before phoned me in the Retreat kitchen.

As soon as I hung up, Wyatt came running through the kitchen, climbed a nearby pine tree, and came running back: "There's a fire! The A-frame is on fire!" The tall trees at the Retreat blocked our view of the column of smoke rising from the small A-frame about three hundred yards away. I went running toward the fire. The little building—one of the first ones built at the Retreat—was blazing like a torch. In the windless air, the flames shot directly upwards.

I noticed with surprise that the surrounding bushes were coated with fire retardant from the borate bomber. Only moments after I arrived, the North San Juan volunteer fire department arrived. How was this possible? Wyatt had phoned them less than five minutes earlier, and we were a good twenty minutes from the fire house. Only after the blaze was extinguished did we learn why the fire fighters appeared so quickly.

Twenty minutes earlier, when one of the children at the Retreat had ridden her bike past the A-frame, there was no sign of a fire. In the ensuing few minutes, the building burst into flame (we have no idea why). At the same moment, a borate bomber was flying over Ananda on its way to a fire in Downieville. Spotting the A-frame fire, the bomber crew called the lookout tower for permission to drop borate on our fire. At the same time the tower contacted our volunteer fire fighters. They were in their truck on the way to the fire before we even realized there was a fire only a

Anandi teaching at
Ananda Village, 1986.

few hundred yards away! The timing was extraordinary. Truly a miracle. I was always impressed that it was at this moment that Swamiji felt to call the Meditation Retreat.

A postscript to this miracle was particularly moving. The next day at our karma yoga session, the retreatants were cleaning up the site. Only ashes remained. But in the nearby bushes, neatly burned around the edges, was the frontispiece photograph of Master from *Autobiography of a Yogi.*

On February 15, 1992, at 4:42 a.m., the Meditation Retreat temple collapsed from wet, heavy snow—known locally as "Sierra cement." At the time the geodesic dome crumpled, Dambara, a resident member, was meditating inside. Seen and heard from inside, Dambara recounted, the sound was of a "freight train thundering in the room, as the front of the temple avalanched down toward me." Miraculously, he was unharmed.

By 7:30 a.m., the Retreat residents gathered in our house to discuss what to do. The phone rang and it was Swamiji. A curious time for him to call. "I left my hat at the Retreat last night. Could you please get it for me?" When Bharat told him what had happened to our temple, he immediately said, "You should use my dome at the Retreat for your temporary temple." Once again, he had known something was happening. Sensing the energy of the temple collapsing, he decided to phone at that unlikely hour.

On April 2, 1999, Swamiji wrote blessing me on my birthday. He also sent what seemed a special blessing during my birthday satsang held at his Crystal Hermitage apartment. His blessings were extraordinary—very deep, expansive, still, impersonal. It was a highlight of my life.

The *Wisdom of Yogananda* Series

IN 2003 I STARTED working again for Crystal Clarity Publishers, this time as an editor. Since so much of Master's unpublished work was now in the public domain, the manager felt that I should create books featuring his writings. I told him that I first needed Swamiji's permission. When Swamiji didn't seem really to understand what the manager had in mind, I proceeded with the project with Swami's assurance that it was probably fine.

The first book, *How to Be Happy All the Time*, felt like a

gift from Master. The editing flowed effortlessly and with a continuous feeling of guidance. I felt Master had done it all. When Swamiji saw the text, he liked it and now understood what the project was. Wanting to give him a copy of the book myself, I went with Bharat to his house. Swami's praise for my work on the book came as a shock. I had felt, more than at any other time I can remember, that I wasn't the doer, that Master had done it all.

When I shared my perspective with Swamiji, he praised me again. When I protested (as if he hadn't heard me the first time), he praised me a third time. Still not understanding, but at least knowing what was appropriate at this point, I said, "Thank you, Swamiji." The incident puzzled me for a long time. Finally it occurred to me that my feeling Master was doing the book through me was the whole point. That is what I had done well—gotten out of the way!

The second *Wisdom* book was *Karma and Reincarnation*. It was more challenging, because the original articles were less well put together than the content chosen for *Happiness*. I think many of the *Happiness* articles had been edited before appearing in the Praecepta lessons. At first Swamiji was enthusiastic; then he ran into some snags and ended up re-editing pretty heavily. I was very grateful; I had myself felt the book needed help. But when I went over his edits, I felt chagrined to see quite a few changes that I should have caught myself—basic things that a careful editor should have noticed.

Because Swamiji was in India at the time, we went there to attend one of his programs. Swamiji behaved differently in India than he did at Ananda Village. At the Village, he covered his divinity with an "I'm-your-friend" mask. Because Indians have a greater understanding of who the spiritual teacher really is, Swamiji was worshipped there as a guru. Though he never took the role to himself, he filled the role in India because it was appropriate to do so for the Indians. When I saw him my first day in India, so strong was the beautiful divinity coming from him that I felt I was looking at God.

Because he'd made so many changes to my work, he wanted to reassure me: "You couldn't have done what I did. You don't have the permission [from Master] to do so." I understood perfectly. In reply, instead of flowing with the divine energy coming from him, I said in a self-deprecating way, "Yes, but I'm sorry for some of the edits I should have caught."

The effect on me of my response was extraordinary. Though my words don't seem particularly negative viewed from the standpoint of our daily culture, in the presence of so much light, what I said seemed to bounce off him and come back to me for what it was: negative energy—not critical energy, simply energy that was not on the wavelength of the high light emanating from Swami. He didn't respond verbally, nor with any facial change. He didn't need to. I understood perfectly.

On that trip to India, there were many classes on Kriya given by our worldwide group of Kriyacharyas. Swamiji was supposed to address us on one of the last days, but he was extremely ill. Because many had flown in from around the world, however, he felt he should appear. Until the last minute, we didn't know what would happen. Then Swami came in with great strength and magnetism. We began with a short meditation. I felt my mind strongly at the spiritual eye. I felt that Swamiji's spiritual eye and mine were the same, united. When, afterwards, I mentioned my experience to Bharat, he said, "That's exactly what I felt." I wonder how many in the audience felt the same thing!

At the end of our 2006 India trip, Bharat and I went to Swami's to deliver him some almond butter. He called us in to say hello. Bharat had been having a hard time with his health during that trip. Swami began praising and praising him. I was looking at Bharat feeling very happy for him, knowing how much Swami's words meant to him. I looked over to Swami; he was staring at me steadily. An odd feeling. I wondered if he'd been testing me to see if I would think, "What about me?" Fortunately I hadn't been! Later, in retrospect, I thought Swami may have sensed in some way my being out of my center in my happiness for Bharat. But at the moment itself, my experience was of being "seen"—not being judged, simply seen.

Swamiji was fully present with all those he met—seeing and accepting them as they truly are.

Swamiji's standard of what was possible was so high, and yet always encouraging, never discouraging.

He was fully present in each moment, aware of everything yet free of opinions. Helping us whenever he could. And in the case of his praise for Bharat, helping two of us at the same time, in different ways!

During our visit, he told us about his recent interview with people from Yogoda Satsanga Society of India, an affiliate of SRF. Antagonistic toward Swamiji, they'd tried to make things difficult for him. Swami's comment: "It could have been an uncomfortable situation, but because I don't exist as a separate reality, there wasn't a problem."

The year after my work on *Karma and Reincarnation*, I edited *Spiritual Marriage*, now called *How to Love and Be Loved*. The project started out well—but then Swamiji, in his words, "massacred" my editing. I learned so much from studying his edits on these two books. Mostly, I learned that he wanted me to make the changes needed— not to leave in quaint ways of speaking simply because Master had done so. He wanted it to read clearly, not quaintly. Though I had personally enjoyed the quaintness, I got the idea.

The fourth book was *How to Be a Success*. As usual, I sent Swamiji a copy. When I saw him next, he said: I didn't read the book. I said I knew that. Then he added, "Now you are getting the hang of it."

After that, I just continued on. For *How to Have Courage, Calmness, and Confidence*, I wanted to include instruction in the Hong-Sau technique. Master had written about the practice, but not in a way that was clear enough for a beginner. I felt the subject was too important for me to edit without Swami's guidance. Though he was very busy, he did the editing, even adding some words that were Master's teachings but not included in the original article. To me he said, "Because I did this so quickly, I want you to go over it to see if it needs editing." I found this article (Master's title was "Breathlessness Is Deathlessness") so valuable that I included it in several of the *Wisdom* books, and sent copies to all our ministers.

When Swamiji was away, he let those of us who were Ananda Lightbearers use his Crystal Hermitage apartment at Ananda Village for our annual seclusions. I myself took many seclusions there. When, as often happened, I was working on one of the *Wisdom* books, I would meditate during the morning and work on the book in the afternoon. The work was a great blessing—trying to listen for Master's guidance, asking if the words he'd used are conveying the meaning he wants to convey, and sometimes feeling more appropriate words pop into my mind. Being in Swamiji's apartment, in his vibration, was ideal.

One of my seclusions came when Swamiji was working on *The Essence of the Bhagavad Gita*. He wanted me to create a glossary for it. Though I had no idea how to do so, I enjoyed the work. Since there was no wi-fi in the apartment, Bharat would come by and get my work, email it to Swamiji, and bring me his corrections. When the *Gita* came out, he gave us the copy numbered "8."

My part in another project for Crystal Clarity was small but very enjoyable. Catherine Kairavi had written *Two Souls, Four Lives*, a portrayal of the life of William the Conqueror and his son Henry I. Feeling that her version needed shortening, Swamiji edited the book himself. My job was to input his edits—a marvelous experience for me. His editing marks are perfectly precise. Though it took some intuition to read his handwriting, I loved doing the inputting. When I took my work to him with a few questions, he commented, "You got thrown into the deep end of the pool!"

Whenever I took seclusion in his apartment, I would always write him to let him know I was there. I didn't ask for his blessing, because I felt that simply his knowing I was there was in itself a blessing.

It was during this time that my mother was at the hospital having a blood transfusion. "I have all this money," she reflected, "and I can't even eat. Maybe I made a mistake. Maybe I should have moved to Ananda." Her words prompted me to ask Swami to pray for her.

The very next day she was bubbling over with joy and love. She had just finished reading *How to Be Happy* and quoted the following sentences: *Objective conditions are always neutral. It is how you react to them that makes them appear sad or happy. . . . Be ever happy inside.*

My mother lived her last two months of life in a blissful state of joy. I feel her glorious transformation was due to Swamiji's prayers.

Donor Dinner Blessings

S OME OF THE highlights of my life at Ananda were the donor dinners Bharat and I attended. These dinners were fundraisers for Crystal Clarity Publishers and we made a commitment with ourselves to attend them to support Swamiji's writing, which was so important to him. The fundraising team created a most heavenly atmosphere, doing everything they could to make all parts of the donor dinner elegant, whether seating us in an exquisite dining room next to the Crystal Hermitage dome or in the garden with fairy lights illumining the setting, flowers everywhere. Dignified waiters (our fellow disciples) served the pre-dinner nonalcoholic wine. The meal itself, created by Nancy Mair (Swamiji later gave her the name Netri), was always extraordinary. But most beautiful of all was the atmosphere created by Swamiji himself. The whole evening was divine.

Swami spoke powerfully and eloquently about each new book featured at one of the donor dinners. When he spoke about *The Rubaiyat of Omar Khayyam Explained* (Yogananda's commentary, which Swami edited, on that great mystical poem), Bharat and I both felt that a great scripture had been born anew.

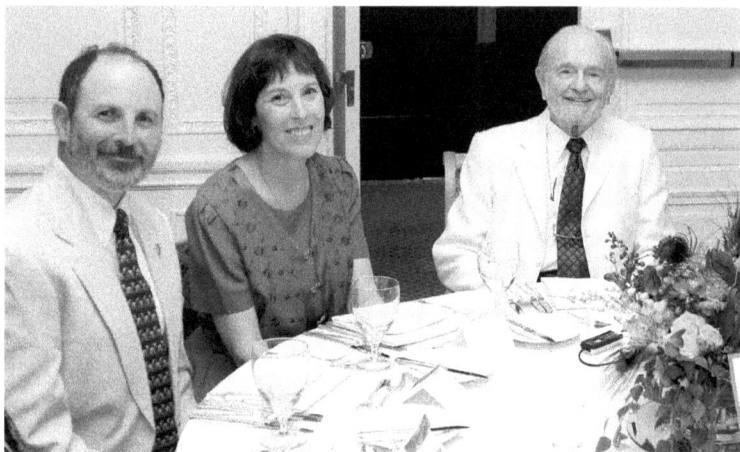

Swami, Anandi, and Bharat at the Palace of Fine Arts Donor Dinner, San Francisco, California.

Yogananda's Kriya Yoga Initiations have their own level of vibration. I don't know how to describe the difference in vibration between these Initiations and the donor dinners. What I can say is that I felt deeply blessed to be able to attend each one.

At one point we traveled to Los Angeles for a program Swamiji was giving, and for the donor dinner before his talk. As we climbed off the rental bus, we learned that Swami had asked that we sit next to him at his table, and that he had explained to the host, "They know how to be quiet" (he didn't want a lot of chatter before his evening talk). Dutifully we told everyone sitting at our table that Swami wanted quiet, but as it turned out, he actively engaged everyone in conversation.

The donor dinners with Swamiji were a sacred blessing. In the room we felt only love and bliss. During 2011's donor dinner, Gurudas of Crystal Clarity spoke of the importance of the *Wisdom of Yogananda* book series. I was a little shocked, feeling that he should emphasize Swami and his books. At the end of the evening, Swami blessed everyone present. After he blessed me, he said, "Thank you for all the work you are doing."

Eternal Friendship

THE LAST WORDS that Swami ever spoke to me came after the 2012 donor dinner: "Thank you for the love you have given me all these years." It was the perfect thing to say to me. It healed any lingering sense of shortcomings on my part, and reminded me that the sole thing I should focus on is loving him. In all my interactions with him, I remember only the love.

A couple of days later, Nayaswami Devi phoned and said, "Swami wants to make you a Kriya Minister, Thursday evening, before his satsang." When Swami arrived for the event, as he stepped out of his car he immediately called for me. His actual blessing of me as a Kriya Minister was relatively brief. Gazing deeply into my eyes, Swamiji said, "Share God's blessings with many people."

Swamiji blessing Anandi at a donor dinner, circa 2010.

2013

THE LAST LETTER I wrote Swami Kriyananda:

Dearest Swamiji,

I write this message today, but the real message is written in my heart and mind every day as I think of you.

Day by day, I am touched by awe, reverence, gratitude, and love for who you are, for what you give to the world, and for what you give to each of us.

Your example of true, egoless discipleship and dedication to serving Master is a priceless gift that I draw from daily. The teachings expressed through your writings and talks increasingly fill me with wonder for their clarity and heart-touching depth.

But what is most precious to me is your amazing love—a never-ending lesson in itself. Love that is so natural, humble, and filled with joy, humor, and understanding. Each of us feels uniquely loved by you.

Swamiji, the last words you said to me were, "Thank you for your love through all these years." Thank *you* for bringing me back always to love.

May I someday fulfill your priceless gifts by giving back to the world what you have given to me.

With love and gratitude,
Anandi

May 20, 2015, Crystal Hermitage

THE DAY BEFORE Swami's body was to be installed in his Moksha Mandir, I was having trouble meditating. But the next morning, in the presence of his body, I felt as if Heaven had opened up. An extraordinary blessing.

April 21, 2019

A T THE MEDITATION honoring Swamiji's moksha [liberation], I felt a strong soul-to-soul bond. The personality challenges that this incarnation presents and presented for Swami were not that important. The important thing is to stay with that soul bond.

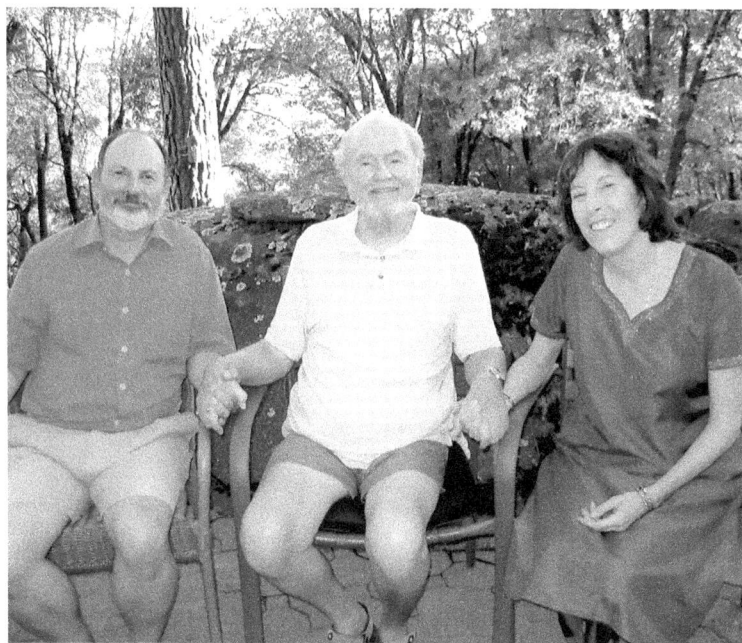

Swamiji visiting Bharat and Anandi in their garden,
Ananda Village, circa 2009.

Paramhansa Yogananda.

PART TWO

*My Inner Life with
Paramhansa Yogananda*

TAKING TO HEART her guru's words—"To those who think me near, I will be near"—Anandi often wrote to Yoganandaji, especially on his birthday (January 5) and during her yearly seclusion. Though Master left his physical body in 1952, Anandi was able to receive his loving response and guidance through moment-to-moment remembrance of him, and through energetically serving his work.

The following excerpts are collected from Anandi's private papers.

December 28, 1975

Dear Master,

The value of writing to you is that it helps me pull together thoughts, pin down amorphous feelings, and arrive at clear-cut directions.

The only relevant thing is how much of my heart I am *giving* to Swamiji.

In the coming year, the habits I want to blast away are worrying that I'm not meditating enough—or as much as or as deeply as others—and comparing myself with others, especially in comparing how much attention Swamiji gives others with how much he gives me.

1986 Letter to Swami

As I came back from Atherton, I felt Master pouring the water of his presence into me. This was beautiful.

March 3, 1991, Winter Renewal Retreat

Dear Master,

Help me to know you truly—to go beyond intermittent connections to a total connection, all the time.

While I was walking and talking to you about what I should "do with my life," I felt that it was You! saying, "Anandi, Anandi, I love you. You are uniquely you and so you are dear. And so are all people uniquely themselves. Feel how much I love each person and relate to him with that love. I am at the heart of everything, loving it because I *am* Love. And each one of you is unique and alike in that love.

May 5, 1991—Dream of Master

Dear Swamiji,

I had another wonderful dream of Master last night—a rare experience. In the dream I was watching a hologram-like film of Master speaking. As he spoke, he seemed to be sending out an energy designed to communicate with his listeners, and to act as a force to turn the thoughts of all the world toward God. After seeing Master, I saw you, and shared this experience with you. I felt thrilled knowing that you had already experienced what I had through Master.

Last week Lennie discovered a mass of some sort on my uterus. . . . I haven't been thinking about it, and that's why I haven't told you sooner. . . . This morning, though, as I thought of you, I thought I should let you know. I can feel your prayers for me always. I am so grateful for your love and guidance and support, which are always available.

January 5, 1996

Dear Swami, dear Master,

Every day let me be thinking about loving God, loving Master, loving Swami, loving Mother and seeing each day as an offering of love. Let me think of each person in my world as God, and show me how I can help each one.

Be with God's joy all the time. Stay centered at the spiritual eye. Be able to absorb self in meditation.

February 9, 1996

Dear Swamiji,

Deepest love and gratitude to you. After twenty-five years at Ananda with you, each day I continue to feel wonder and gratitude for the miracle that has come through you to me and to the whole world. It is not possible to thank you enough.

Nayaswami Anandi teaching meditation at the Wanderlust Yoga Festival, Palisades Tahoe (then called "Squaw Valley"), circa 2016.

January 5, 2002, Birthday Card for Yogananda

Master,

I long to apply myself in meditation—not leaning on excuses for why I am not concentrating in this moment.

I long to see every moment as coming from you—pain, discomfort, slights, opportunities to be "left out." Each is a great blessing: a chance to express joy and God-attunement, and to be victorious.

Master, I long to remember that you are the Guru, the Giver, and that my role is to receive gratefully and joyfully—not to tell you how my life should be.

I long to be centered in God, to be relaxed in my trust in your wise, omniscient guidance and love, and to see the God in others.

Above all I long to be kind in thoughts—to others and to myself. Help me to be a channel for your goodness.

I offer to you the personal insecurities that come between me and my complete trust in Swami's love. Bless me with ever deepening love for you and for your channel.

My blessed Master,

Thoughts of you fill my heart today. Two or three weeks ago I felt you looking thoughtfully at me, and inwardly I heard you say, "The quirks have disappeared." I think so too. When a ship is taken into pure water the barnacles drop off. Similarly, when God allows a devotee to live in the pure spiritual water that surrounds a guru, faults disappear without effort.

November 2004, Seclusion in Swamiji's Apartment, Ananda Village

Happiness is at the spiritual eye. Remember to keep offering energy there and to keep positive expectations.

Focus on being a manifestation of the Dreamer. I may be better or worse than others, but no matter how much worse I am, I am still made of the Dreamer. Keep in mind His love and happiness always. This is how to find that impersonal place I'm looking for.

See ALL others as made of the Dreamer also. No competition. Just appreciating the beautiful expression of God through all my friends.

2007—Anandi's Spiritual Goals

Every morning focus at the point between the eyebrows and in the spine; try to be there as much as possible. Think of Swamiji's calmness and graciousness; he's never rushed and never thrown off his center.

Meditate often on how he loves people—seeing all people as they ARE, with no judgment about any difficulties they might cause. They just ARE; their reality is the God within them. There's no need to put anyone on a pedestal. Simply appreciate all from your center; view all with kindness and deep appreciation.

There's no need to compete or compare oneself with anyone, or to worry that others are better than you; simply appreciate the beauty of each person— whether "higher or lower" on the social scale.

If you trust in God, you will find that, by asking Him for help, He will do everything you ask of Him, provided you ask with faith. Don't plead with Him. Say, rather, "This is what I am trying to accomplish for You. I need Your strength, and Your guidance. I'll do what I can, but You must do the rest."

2007 Seclusion

Master, You are always with me. I can choose to absorb myself in all my little battles and litany of faults, or I can place them in Your hands.

This seclusion has been blessed by working on Your book *How to Be a Success*. It is such a beautiful book, filled with wonderfully helpful thoughts for overcoming negative habits, such as the habit of failure.

This morning I thought that perhaps I should start a small moneymaking scheme to earn money for the Ananda lawsuit. Its theme would be developing the qualities You speak of in *How to Be a Success*.

Then the smoke in my brain cleared, and I thought, my focus in this life is on loving God and Guru.

Keeping my mind with You is the most important focus for my willpower—staying with joy and largeness instead of with smallness. This is what it's about. At the same time, building on the inspiration of this retreat, I want to put better, fresher, more dynamic energy into whatever is in front of me.

But I have to keep coming back to the moment: to You. My affirmation this morning was not something like "I am brave, etc." but "You will win this battle"—tuning in to the reality that You are doing it all. In this attunement is victory. God is the doer, through me. His power will win over the nattering voice of self-doubt.

So, You are HERE. Challenging as it is for me to relax my body, to focus my mind in stillness, You are HERE. Life is not what it seems; it's important to remember that this life is all God's dream. The very fabric of life is God and Guru. We are never away from You. Meditation is our best attempt; we need to go into meditation remembering, You are already here. I don't have to attain You, only more and more deeply to remember You.

2008 Seclusion in Swami's Apartment at Ananda Village

Dear Master,

Thank you for this amazing opportunity to seclude in Swamiji's shrine, the most perfect place on earth, truly, with him here and You here. Coming into seclusion, I was once again very aware of the blocks within me, one of the most intractable, a feeling of separation from You and from Swamiji. I worried whether I was worthy to take seclusion in his apartment. Then, at one point, I felt Swamiji saying within me: I WANT to help you, I WANT you to take seclusion there.

The trip to Crystal Hermitage was proof of a very special blessing. On Monday (the day I moved in) the road was covered in snow and extremely slippery. Lalita rode with us; Bharat did the driving. We made the mistake of driving to the lower Crystal Hermitage parking lot instead of the Ayodhya lot. The car became stuck halfway down. We carried what I needed the rest of the way, and walked back up with a shovel to dig ourselves out. We all prayed; Bharat managed to free the car and drive up to the top. I walked back down to Swami's apartment, and Bharat and Lalita drove out via Sage's Road—more of an adventure than they had expected. The road was blocked by snow-laden tree branches; so much snow built up on the car's front windows that at times Bharat couldn't see out. The way out to Tyler Foote Road was hilly and slippery. When I heard the story, I felt Your loving blessings; Bharat told me later that he had also felt blessed and protected.

Once I was somewhat settled, I sat to meditate. I could feel the divine presence at the spiritual eye; all

I wanted was to be with that presence. Meditation was effortless.

All my concerns vanished in superconsciousness. Here is my focus for this seclusion and from now on. Joy and love. "I have burnt my past."

I offer my limitations to You.

Master, I cannot change myself by myself. I have to hand myself over with love and trust. What is, simply is. All personality is foam on the surface of the sea. Let me live in the ocean deeps.

My walk this afternoon was full of Your joyous presence. The flow of our energy must be toward the spiritual eye all the time. Any negativity pulls the energy away.

In order to feel Your presence, I have been focusing on physically imagining You as my body.

I have only one job: to keep my consciousness with You, to grow in love and joy and attunement. To keep my eye on the ball, in the present. To try to be connected to You in love and joy, and to share that connection through service at Ananda. The big picture is wholly up to You.

The spiritual eye is the gateway to infinite, divine love. "The flow of our energy must be toward the spiritual eye—all the time," Anandi has written. When we center our consciousness there, the heart's feelings channel God's love through it out to all the world. When Anandi met with and counseled others, she would attune inwardly to the energy at her spiritual eye and spine, then project Master's healing energy to whoever was in front of her. She created this simple poster—which was placed on the desk in her office—to remind herself to live *from* the spiritual eye.

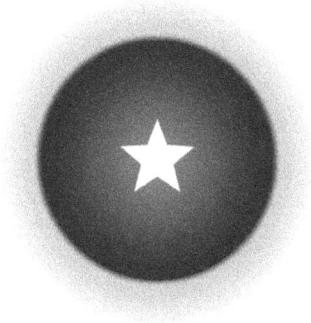

So steadily did Nayaswami Anandi direct her energy toward the spiritual eye that at times she felt Swamiji's spiritual eye and hers were united.

2014 Seclusion, Swamiji's Dome, Meditation Retreat

A**FTER READING** "The Heart of a Stone Image" in *Autobiography of a Yogi* and contemplating Roma's deep devotion and even-minded love and generosity, I stepped onto Swamiji's deck in the early morning and felt, "Everything I see is the body of Divine Mother. Every person, including me, is part of Her body."

Remember: Always step back into Divine Mother's presence and see all as part of Her.

Date Unknown

Dear Master,

Deeply inspiring for me is to think of the great beauty that is in others—instead of wishing I could be like others or worrying that I'm not, to feel in my center that others are also I. Instead of dwelling on what I am not, to feel a joyful expansion of consciousness toward goodness.

My goal is more and more to feel my love for You guiding me. To ask, What do You want me to do now, Master? How can I give each person Your love and joy!

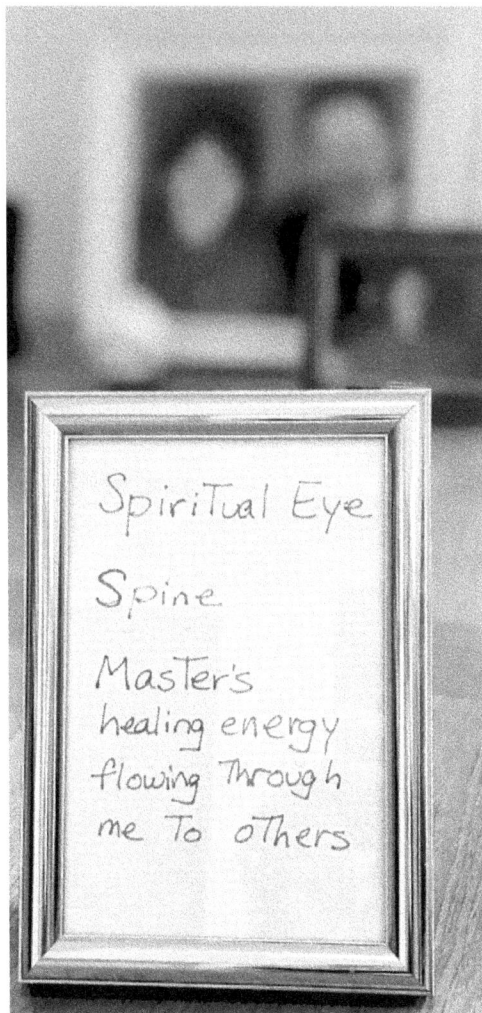

Anandi placed this simple poster on her community desk to remind her to channel the healing energy of the spiritual eye to everyone she met.

PART THREE

Infinite Freedom

Divine love is the active expression of divine bliss. Seva and Anandi enjoying their bliss together, circa 2005.

What Goes, What Stays

By Nayaswami Jyotish

Touch of Light Blog, February 3, 2022

IN THE LAST TWO MONTHS we have seen two great souls depart this world. Nayaswami Seva passed away on November 14, and we just held an Astral Ascension Ceremony for Nayaswami Anandi, who passed away five days ago. Anandi had been a member of Ananda and our dear friend for more than fifty years. The talk given at the ceremony by her lifelong husband, Bharat, was particularly touching.

Yet, as all of us must do, these friends have moved on to the astral world. What remains? What is permanent? Memories may stay alive for a time but only God's eternal qualities stand unchanged by the crashing waves of maya. I would like to look past Anandi's personality and touch on a few of the qualities that she manifested, in ways that were particularly inspiring to me:

Everything was God-centered. Anandi was very clear that the purpose of this life was to find spiritual liberation, and she shaped her life around that goal. She was always listening for God's whispers drawing us back to the bliss of our true Self. Though she held many different jobs and roles and gave countless classes and talks, she never identified herself with what she did.

We spent a lot of time working together with her, walking together, and connecting about little things in the way true friends do. She never judged people, nor had any tendency to get into negativity or gossip. I remember one walk where the conversation started to drift toward some problems and negative qualities of one of the guests. Anandi quickly said, "Let's talk about something more uplifting."

A lesson from Anandi: Mold your life around your search for God.

Selflessness expressed by serving others. There were hundreds of people whose lives were uplifted and changed by talking with her. She spent a lot of time talking with visitors, and never considered it as anything special. But they did! Her husband, Bharat, said that they received over a thousand notes of appreciation after her passing. She was extremely humble in the true sense of the word: not thinking about herself. Because of that, she was able to allow the space for people to feel safe enough to open up the deeper parts of themselves.

A lesson from Anandi: Dissolve your ego through humbly serving others.

Persistence. When Anandi took up a task, you knew that she would see it through to the end no matter what it took.

As an example, she created the wonderful eight-book series, *Wisdom of Yogananda*, compilations of Master's teachings on various topics. Just think of the countless hours it must have taken to study, extract, and categorize those wonderful quotes.

A lesson from Anandi: Stick with the job until it is done. And, your main job is yourself.

Joy and good humor. The name, Anandi, that Swami Kriyananda gave her means "joy." And there was a stream of joy and good humor that flowed beneath the surface, always ready to well up in a laugh, a quick, amused comment, or a smile. Of all the things of value that Anandi shared with me, I think that her joy was the most important. It is the very essence of who she was, who we all are.

A lesson from Anandi: Live joyfully.

These are just a few of the many eternal qualities of God that Anandi manifested. And, while her body and personality may be gone, the examples from her life are forever woven into the fabric of Ananda. Soon we will have a memorial service where friends from around the world can share more stories. It is sure to be filled with God's light and joy. That is to say it will be filled with Anandi.

In joy,
Nayaswami Jyotish

Anandi's face radiated love.

Expanding Love

Nayaswami Anandi's Transition

By Nayaswami Bharat

A WEEK BEFORE SHE PASSED, Anandi told me, "My heart has been at peace since the beginning." When she heard her cancer was untreatable, she smiled and quietly cheered, "Hurray!"—so eager was she to go with our Gurus to God. Minutes after leaving the body, her face became serene and radiant. A pervading aura of bliss spoke of her victory over physical existence.

During her last week, she remarked gratefully, "The love that has come our way through the community [and all of Ananda] has been tremendous. My only wish is that I could give back to people to share with them the love and gratitude I feel for each person. I hope they already know."

Anandi brought great joy and love to everyone she met. Days before her death, the veil separating her from the astral world seemed to disappear, and her ability to share Master's bliss seemed unlimited by time and space. The shift from being *in* the physical body to being *outside* it, coincided with reports of Anandi blessing others at a distance. Nayaswami Narayan wrote during this transitional time, "My prayers have changed: I used to pray *for* Anandi, now I pray *to* her."

Swamiji wrote, "Love is a link between people; it draws them together, until their affection merges at last in the great ocean of divine love." Anandi's mature love for Swamiji drew them together, just as we are drawn together by Anandi's love for us and our love for her.

When death approaches, Swamiji urges, the sincere devotee should make an extra effort to focus on God alone. In respect for Anandi's time alone with God, Ananda friends created a meditation area overlooking her bedroom—a way to be nearby yet not so close as to distract her.

As Jivani meditated in this special area one cold winter morning, Anandi appeared to her:

> After meditating for about thirty minutes [Jivani writes], I felt very inward and still. Suddenly, in my mind's eye, I saw Anandi standing in front of me smiling her big vibrant smile; she said "hello" in the way she always does. She was in her nayaswami robes. I greeted her back and she sat next to me. It all seemed very natural and very real.
>
> Anandi told me, "I like to come here and sit with everyone. It's very sweet. I'm very touched by everyone's love." After a long pause, she continued, "You know I'll always be around, like the others, helping everyone."

Then she turned to me and said, "You will be helping everyone here too."

Then we sat for a while as the sun rose. I felt my soul expand with her enormous loving presence to the gates of the astral realm. There were tears of joy and gratitude. All sadness of her leaving evaporated. I could feel the curtain between the two worlds very thin.

"After my Kriya practice," Avanti, a Finnish Kriyaban, wrote us, "I felt a sudden presence with me. It was warm and loving and I intuitively knew it was Anandi. Since she was the one who'd led my online Kriya Initiation, her blessing felt particularly special, as though she was giving me reassurance that I was doing okay. At the time, I was often just trying to keep track of the steps of Kriya, and very rarely felt anything deep afterward. The next day I found out during Sunday service that on Saturday there had been a celebration of her life at Ananda Village."

During Anandi's Astral Ascension Ceremony in Assisi, Italy, one woman, though she had not known Anandi directly, felt her heart bursting with gratitude for Anandi; rising to speak, she felt enveloped in Anandi's presence, then saw her standing beside her, watching her lovingly.

On each of the two days preceding her passing, as I meditated at Lotus Lake, Anandi shared with me her state of inner freedom. In the beginning of each meditation,

I saw the crown chakra's violet circle surrounding its liberating white tunnel; then I lost body consciousness. The same experience came again two months later. I feel Anandi was sharing her present state of consciousness in order to encourage me (and all of us) on our way to God.

After receiving a saintly blessing from Anandi, Dayanand wrote me the following letter:

> The day after Anandi's passing . . . I felt her spirit visit me very strongly. [It] just came out of the blue. And it was very sweet and light: like Anandi, but so much more so.

> And she sent me something else important at that same time that I thought you should know.

> In the 1980s, when I was in Sorrento, Italy, a friend told me he was going to visit the Catholic stigmatist Natuzza (the one who recommended that Swami and Rosanna marry). I sent Natuzza a message, and when my friend returned days later with her answer, for hours that day I smelled roses in the room. I thought maybe someone was wearing a strong cologne, but my friend told me, after I'd smelled that, that Natuzza sometimes sent people a blessing called "the odor of sanctity." Padre Pio used to send the same sweet odor.

I thought you would want to know that our beloved Anandi sent the same astral fragrance that great saints have sent to people. Her spirit that day was so light. I was so moved and touched that she would visit me and bless me like that.

Nayaswami Devi has several times this past year reminded me that "Anandi is helping us." I myself, like many others, have experienced her help. On January 13, 2023, while I was completing this book for Anandi, in a superconscious dream-vision Anandi and I walked together for a long time, sharing the vibration of our mutual love, all the while immersed in a vibrant stillness. From time to time, one of us would speak a few words about our new, higher relationship in God. As the dream was ending, and we were to go our separate ways, Anandi said quietly, and knowingly, "Love is the only thing that exists."

Earlier she had said, "I will continue to help people here on earth."

Many readers of this book, I feel, share Anandi's experience of discipleship and service to the guru. Anandi's and my prayer for you is that your heartfelt dedication and expanding love bring you quickly to God.

Paramhansa Yogananda and the Ananda Kriya Gurus have given us this sacred promise: "You must be true to yourself and to us; we are in earnest . . . and are resolved to show you that cosmic consciousness and divine power are attainable in one life, if you properly and continuously cooperate in this divine endeavor."

In divine love,
Nayaswami Bharat

Nayaswami Bharat and Anandi leading Sunday service, circa 2018.

Learn More About Anandi

- Her inspirational lectures and writings
- Her Astral Ascension Ceremony
- The *Wisdom of Yogananda* book series

  crystalclarity.com/anandi

APPENDIX A

Stories of Anandi's Transition
by Fellow Disciples

Irene Schulman

THE DAY WAS dawning and it was quite chilly. I had just listened to the community message that Anandi had passed away. I felt I needed to take a walk to help process what had happened. It was so early that the light was just coming up on the horizon. Everything was calm and quiet. As I walked on the road by the Cornells' house, I decided to meditate at the simple altar outside Anandi's bedroom.

There were two small benches (one in front of the other). I chose to sit in the one farther from the house. I wrapped myself up in a cozy, warm blanket that was left for us to use while meditating. I closed my eyes and began to center myself by sending love to Anandi. A couple minutes later I heard the sound of someone coming closer and closer to me. I imagined it was a person who also wanted to meditate. The footsteps came right past me and paused. Assuming it was someone who knew me well and wanted to sit next to me, I opened my eyes.

To my amazement, a doe stood right next to me. Her face was about six inches from mine. Her big beautiful eyes were looking right at me. She turned to leave, took a step, then looked back again before disappearing into the forest.

Nayaswami Padma

A few days after Anandi's passing, I had a vivid dream of Nayaswamis Seva, Lila, and Anandi enjoying one another "on the other side." The veil seemed very thin. God is our only reality.

Nayaswami Kabir

Dear Brother Bharat,

I want to share with you a dream I had of Anandi the day she passed into the higher Light. The dream took place just two hours before she left her body.

In the dream, which may have been a kind of astral vision, Anandi was lying on her bed; we all were aware that she was preparing to leave her body. She was fully awake and present, her body slightly sitting up with her head gently resting on the hand of her bent left arm, with her elbow on the bed. The room was bright and full of light. Two others were there with me, both to my right. Although I could not see them, I could feel their presence. I didn't know who they were nor did I hear them speak.

Anandi's eyes were bright. Her body looked forty years younger, her age when I first met her at Ananda Village. She was speaking to us about her leaving the body. I was amazed to see her looking so young, centered, alert, focused, and aware of all that was happening to her. And then I said aloud in the dream, with joyful enthusiasm and for all to know:

"Anandi is NOT dying! She is more alive than I have ever seen her!"

Nayaswami Anandi, six years old, lying in the same posture as in Nayaswami Kabir's vision moments before her transition: "Anandi's body looked like she was in her twenties — relaxed and happy."

Seraphina Walker

This morning (early February, 2022) I was having difficulty meditating. I was restless; a parade of thoughts was passing through my mind. While practicing Kriya, I stopped for a moment, took a couple of breaths, and had a little mental chat with Anandi. I thanked her deeply for the beautiful Kriya ceremony that I was honored to share with her in 2015, my first Kriya Initiation.

Remembering the experience, I asked Anandi—now that she has a greater, expanded consciousness—could she help me with my Kriya practice this morning? Soon I felt a blissful energy coming in with the breeze through a window in the Temple. An uplifting and tranquil presence surrounded me, which became stronger and stronger. The spiritual eye was bright and vivid. I felt tremendous peace in and all around me.

Nayaswami Dhyana

(A written message to Anandi on January 20, 2022—ten days before her passing.)

You helped me in many ways on the path—mainly with the example of your total surrender and discipleship that must be written in the ether for eternity. Few have lived discipleship like that. Master and Swamiji must be so pleased with you.

"I try always to tune into the underlying reality of our souls
and the deep kinship we share." —Anandi

APPENDIX B

A Divine Marriage

"Anandi's marriage to Bharat Joseph Cornell was lived in the same spirit with which she did everything. When they were together, you could feel their deep, unspoken love and appreciation for each other, and see the joy that twinkled in their eyes at being together." —Nayaswami Devi

IN A 2018 NOTE Anandi expressed the divine soul bond she shares with Bharat:

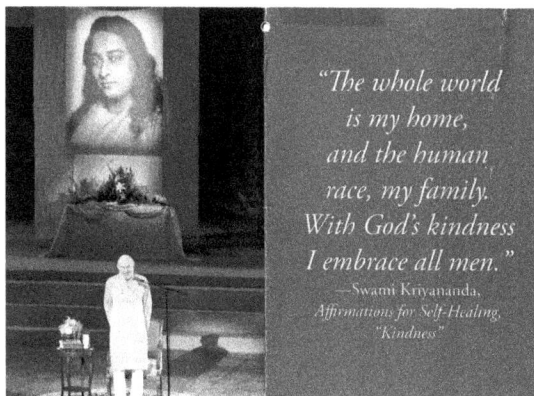

A reproduction of the card that Anandi gave to Bharat with her handwritten message inside.

To My Beloved Friend,

On so many levels, Master's gift to me of marriage to you has blessed me more than I could ever have imagined.

The joy of sharing nature, nature adventures, tuning in to trees and animals, and life force in nature, more than I could have imagined.

The joy of sharing our love for God and helping each other as we share this Ray through our ministry together.

The blessing of having a friend who truly loves me and sees the highest in me.

* Not in order of importance!

To My Beloved Friend,

On so many levels, Master's gift to me of marriage to you has blessed me more than I could ever have imagined.

The joy of sharing nature, nature adventures, tuning in to trees and animals, and life force in nature, more than I can imagine.

The joy of sharing our love for God and helping each other as we share this Ray through our ministry together.

The blessing of having a friend who truly loves me and sees the highest in me.

* Not in order of importance!

The tremendous fun and laughter we share no matter where we are.

The shared understanding of life—coming from a similar perspective anchored in the wisdom of Master and Swamiji.

Being around your vibration—deeply centered in the spine, calm, impartial, wise, gentle, kind, loving all. Your wisdom comes through everything you do.

May your footsteps lead you unerringly to the Goal.

with love,

with joy and gratitude,
with divine friendship,
Anandi

I always try to tune in to the underlying place of our souls and the deep kinship we share.

The tremendous fun and
laughter we can share no
matter where we are.

The shared understanding of
life — coming from a similar
perspective anchored in the
wisdom of Master ad Swamiji.

Being around your vibration
— deeply centered in the spine,
calm, impartial, wise,
gentle, kind, loving all. Your
wisdom comes through everything
you do.

May your footsteps lead you
unerringly to the Goal.

with love,
with joy and gratitude,
with divine friendship,

Anandi

I always try to tune into the underlying
place of our souls and the deep kinship we
share.

With Divine Friendship, Nayaswami Anandi

About Paramhansa Yogananda

Born in 1893, Yogananda was the first yoga master of India to take up permanent residence in the West.

Yogananda arrived in America in 1920 and traveled throughout the country on what he called his "spiritual campaigns." Hundreds of thousands filled the largest halls in major cities to see the yoga master from India. Yogananda continued to lecture and write up to his passing in 1952.

Yogananda's initial impact on Western culture was truly impressive. His lasting spiritual legacy has been even greater. His *Autobiography of a Yogi*, first published in 1946, helped launch a spiritual revolution in the West. Translated into more than fifty languages, it remains a best-selling spiritual classic to this day.

Before embarking on his mission, Yogananda received this admonition from his teacher, Swami Sri Yukteswar: "The West is high in material attainments but lacking in spiritual understanding. It is God's will that you play a role in teaching mankind the value of balancing the material with an inner, spiritual life."

In addition to *Autobiography of a Yogi*, Yogananda's spiritual legacy includes music, poetry, and extensive commentaries on the Bhagavad Gita, the *Rubaiyat* of Omar Khayyam, and the Christian Bible, showing the principles of Self-realization as the unifying truth underlying all true religions. Through his teachings and his Kriya Yoga path millions of people around the world have found a new way to connect personally with God.

His mission, however, was far broader than all this. It was to help usher the whole world into Dwapara Yuga, the new Age of Energy in which we live. "Someday," Swami Kriyananda wrote, "I believe he will be seen as the *avatar* of Dwapara Yuga: the way shower for a new age."

About Swami Kriyananda

A prolific author, accomplished composer, playwright, and artist, and a world-renowned spiritual teacher, Swami Kriyananda (1926-2013) referred to himself simply as close disciple of the great God-realized master, Paramhansa Yogananda. He met his guru at the age of twenty-two, and served him during the last four years of the Master's life. He dedicated the rest of his life to sharing Yogananda's teachings throughout the world.

Kriyananda was born in Romania of American parents, and educated in Europe, England, and the United States. Philosophically and artistically inclined from youth, he soon came to question life's meaning and society's values. During a period of intense inward reflection, he discovered Yogananda's *Autobiography of a Yogi*, and immediately traveled three thousand miles from New York to California to meet the Master, who accepted him as a monastic disciple. Yogananda appointed him as the head of the monastery, authorized him to teach and give Kriya Initiation in his name, and entrusted him with the missions of writing, teaching, and creating what he called "world brotherhood colonies."

Kriyananda founded the first such community, Ananda Village, in the Sierra Nevada foothills of Northern California in 1968. Ananda is recognized as one of the most successful intentional communities in the world today. It has served as a model for other such communities that he founded subsequently in the United States, Europe, and India.

FURTHER EXPLORATIONS

CRYSTAL CLARITY PUBLISHERS

If you enjoyed this title, Crystal Clarity Publishers invites you to deepen your spiritual life through many additional resources based on the teachings of Paramhansa Yogananda. We offer books, e-books, audiobooks, yoga and meditation videos, and a wide variety of inspirational and relaxation music composed by Swami Kriyananda.

See a listing of books below, visit our secure website for a complete online catalog, or place an order for our products.

crystalclarity.com
800.424.1055 | clarity@crystalclarity.com
1123 Goodrich Blvd. | Commerce, CA 90022

ANANDA WORLDWIDE

Crystal Clarity Publishers is the publishing house of Ananda, a worldwide spiritual movement founded by Swami Kriyananda, a direct disciple of Paramhansa Yogananda. Ananda offers resources and support for your spiritual journey through meditation instruction, webinars, online virtual community, email, and chat.

Ananda has more than 150 centers and meditation groups in over 45 countries, offering group guided meditations, classes and teacher training in meditation and yoga, and many other resources.

In addition, Ananda has developed eight residential communities in the US, Europe, and India. Spiritual communities are places where people live together in a spirit of cooperation and friendship, dedicated to a common goal. Spirituality is practiced in all areas of daily life: at school, at work, or in the home. Many Ananda communities offer internships during which one can stay and experience spiritual community firsthand.

For more information about Ananda communities or meditation groups near you, please visit **ananda.org** or call 530.478.7560.

THE EXPANDING LIGHT RETREAT
The Expanding Light is the largest retreat center in the world to share exclusively the teachings of Paramhansa Yogananda. Situated in the Ananda Village community near Nevada City, California, the center offers the opportunity to experience spiritual life in a contemporary ashram setting. The varied, year-round schedule of classes and programs on yoga, meditation, and spiritual practice includes Karma Yoga, personal retreat, spiritual travel, and online learning. Large groups are welcome.

The Ananda School of Yoga & Meditation offers certified yoga, yoga therapist, spiritual counselor, and meditation teacher trainings.

The teaching staff has years of experience practicing Kriya Yoga meditation and all aspects of Paramhansa Yogananda's teachings. You may come for a relaxed personal renewal, participating in ongoing activities as much or as little as you wish. The serene mountain setting, supportive staff, and delicious vegetarian meals provide an ideal environment for a truly meaningful stay, be it a brief respite or an extended spiritual vacation.

For more information, please visit **expandinglight.org** or call 800.346.5350.

ANANDA MEDITATION RETREAT

Set amidst seventy-two acres of beautiful meditation gardens and wild forest in Northern California's Sierra foothills, the Ananda Meditation Retreat is an ideal setting for a rejuvenating, inner experience.

The Meditation Retreat has been a place of deep meditation and sincere devotion for over fifty years. Long before that, the Native American Maidu tribe held this to be sacred land. The beauty and presence of the Divine are tangibly felt by all who visit here.

Studies show that being in nature and using techniques such as forest bathing can significantly reduce stress and blood pressure while strengthening your immune system, concentration, and level of happiness. The Meditation Retreat is the perfect place for quiet immersion in nature.

Plan a personal retreat, enjoy one of the guided retreats, or choose from a variety of programs led by the caring and joyful staff.

For more information or to place your reservation, please visit **meditationretreat.org**, email **meditationretreat@ananda.org**, or call 530.478.7557.

❁ ❁ ❁ ❁ ❁

The Original Writings of Paramhansa Yogananda

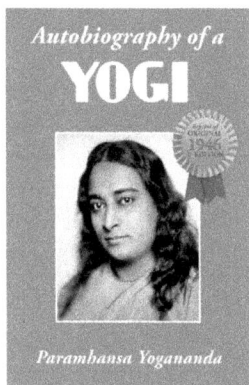

THE ORIGINAL 1946 UNEDITED EDITION OF YOGANANDA'S SPIRITUAL MASTERPIECE

AUTOBIOGRAPHY OF A YOGI
Paramhansa Yogananda

Autobiography of a Yogi is one of the world's most acclaimed spiritual classics, with millions of copies sold. Named one of the Best 100 Spiritual Books of the twentieth century, this book helped launch and continues to inspire a spiritual awakening throughout the Western world.

Yogananda was the first yoga master of India whose mission brought him to settle and teach in the West. His firsthand account of his life experiences in India includes childhood revelations, stories of his visits to saints and masters, and long-secret teachings of yoga and Self-realization that he first made available to the Western reader.

This reprint of the original 1946 edition is free from textual changes made after Yogananda's passing in 1952. This updated edition includes bonus materials: the last chapter that Yogananda wrote in 1951, also without posthumous changes, the eulogy Yogananda wrote for Gandhi, and a new foreword and afterword by Swami Kriyananda, one of Yogananda's close, direct disciples.

Also available in Spanish and Hindi from Crystal Clarity Publishers.

SCIENTIFIC HEALING AFFIRMATIONS
Paramhansa Yogananda

Yogananda's 1924 classic, reprinted here, is a pioneering work in the fields of self-healing and self-transformation. He explains that words are crystallized thoughts and have life-changing power when spoken with conviction, concentration, willpower, and feeling. Yogananda offers far more than mere suggestions for achieving positive attitudes. He shows how to impregnate words with spiritual force to shift habitual thought patterns of the mind and create a new personal reality.

Added to this text are over fifty of Yogananda's well-loved "Short Affirmations," taken from issues of *East-West* and *Inner Culture* magazines from 1932 to 1942. This little book will be a treasured companion on the road to realizing your highest, divine potential.

METAPHYSICAL MEDITATIONS
Paramhansa Yogananda

Metaphysical Meditations is a classic collection of meditation techniques, visualizations, affirmations, and prayers from the great yoga master, Paramhansa Yogananda. The meditations given are of three types: those spoken to the individual consciousness, prayers or demands addressed to God, and affirmations that bring us closer to the Divine.

Select a passage that meets your specific need and speak each word slowly and purposefully until you become absorbed in its inner meaning. At the bedside, by the meditation seat, or while traveling—one can choose no better companion than *Metaphysical Meditations*.

The Wisdom of Yogananda *series*

Paramhansa Yogananda's timeless wisdom is offered here in an approachable, easy-to-read format. The writings of the Master are presented with minimal editing to capture his expansive and compassionate wisdom, his sense of fun, and his practical spiritual guidance.

HOW TO BE HAPPY ALL THE TIME
The Wisdom of Yogananda, volume 1

Yogananda explains everything needed to lead a happier, more fulfilling life. Topics include: looking for happiness in the right places; choosing to be happy; tools, techniques, and methods for achieving happiness; sharing happiness with others; and balancing success with happiness.

KARMA AND REINCARNATION
The Wisdom of Yogananda, volume 2

Yogananda reveals the reality of karma, death, reincarnation, and the afterlife. With clarity and simplicity, he makes the mysterious understandable: why we see a world of suffering and inequality; what happens at death and after death; the purpose of reincarnation; and how to handle the challenges we face in our lives.

HOW TO LOVE AND BE LOVED
The Wisdom of Yogananda, volume 3

Yogananda shares practical guidance and fresh insight on relationships of all types: how to cure friendship-ending habits; how to choose the right partner; the role of sex in marriage; how to conceive a spiritually oriented child; the solutions to problems that arise in marriage; and the Universal Love at the heart of all relationships.

HOW TO BE A SUCCESS
The Wisdom of Yogananda, volume 4

The Attributes of Success, Yogananda's original booklet on reaching one's goals, is included here along with his other writings on success: how to develop habits of success and eradicate habits of failure; thriving in the right job; how to build willpower and magnetism; and finding the true purpose of one's life.

HOW TO HAVE COURAGE, CALMNESS, AND CONFIDENCE
The Wisdom of Yogananda, volume 5

A master at helping people change and grow, Yogananda shows how to transform one's life: dislodge negative thoughts and depression; uproot fear and thoughts of failure; cure nervousness and systematically eliminate worry from life; and overcome anger, sorrow, oversensitivity, and a host of other troublesome emotions.

Winner of the 2011 International Book Award for Best Self-Help Title

HOW TO ACHIEVE GLOWING HEALTH AND VITALITY
The Wisdom of Yogananda, volume 6

Yogananda explains principles that promote physical health and overall well-being, mental clarity, and inspiration in one's spiritual life. He offers practical, wide-ranging, and fascinating suggestions on having more energy and living a radiantly healthy life. Readers will discover the priceless Energization Exercises for rejuvenating the body and mind, the fine art of conscious relaxation, and helpful diet tips for health and beauty.

HOW TO AWAKEN YOUR TRUE POTENTIAL
The Wisdom of Yogananda, volume 7

With compassion, humor, and deep understanding of human psychology, Yogananda offers instruction on releasing limitations to access the power of mind and heart. Discover your hidden resources and be empowered to choose a life with greater meaning, purpose, and joy.

THE MAN WHO REFUSED HEAVEN
The Wisdom of Yogananda, volume 8

Why is humor so deeply appreciated? Laughter is one of the great joys of life. Joy is fundamental to who we are. The humor in this book is taken from Yogananda's writings. Also included are experiences with the Master that demonstrate his playful spirit.

HOW TO FACE LIFE'S CHANGES
The Wisdom of Yogananda, volume 9

Changes come not to destroy us, but to help us grow in understanding and learn the lessons we must to reach our highest potential. Guided by Yogananda, tap into the changeless joy of your soul-nature, empowering you to move through life fearlessly and with an open heart. Learn to accept change as the reality of life; face change in relationships, finances, and health with gratitude; and cultivate key attitudes like fearlessness, non-attachment, and willpower.

HOW TO SPIRITUALIZE YOUR LIFE
The Wisdom of Yogananda, volume 10

Yogananda answers a wide range of questions from truth seekers, sharing his teachings and insights on how to be successful in the everyday world and in one's spiritual life. Addressing financial, physical, mental, emotional, and spiritual challenges, he explains how best to expand one's consciousness and live life to the fullest. Compiled from his articles, lessons, and handwritten letters, this tenth volume in the Wisdom of Yogananda series was written in a question-and-answer format, well suited to both individual and group study.

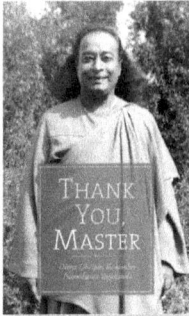

THANK YOU, MASTER
Direct Disciples Remember Paramhansa Yogananda
Hare Krishna Ghosh, Meera Ghosh, Peggy Deitz

Anyone who has read and loved *Autobiography of a Yogi* will be delighted to find this treasure of personal experiences and heartfelt remembrances of Paramhansa Yogananda by three of his direct disciples.

Stories from Yogananda's family members, Hare Krishna Ghosh and Meera Ghosh, who became disciples as teenagers, take the reader on pilgrimage to India to the sacred places and miraculous moments shared with this great yogi. The stories of Peggy Deitz transport one to Yogananda's ashram in California and his life with devotees in America.

Whether humorous or miraculous, mundane or divine, these firsthand accounts from close disciples bring to life the experience of being in Yogananda's presence. They give insight into the profound love with which he guided each individual.

Touch of Light *series*

In their popular weekly blog, A Touch of Light, the authors share spiritual teachings both practical and profound, drawing on the wisdom and the spirit of their guru, Paramhansa Yogananda, and of his direct disciple—and their lifelong teacher—Swami Kriyananda. Collected in these books is the complete series of these blogs to date, starting from the very first blog published in July 2013.

TOUCH OF DIVINE WISDOM
Living the Teachings of Paramhansa Yogananda

Read the wisdom gained through over fifty years on the spiritual path, offering the keys for how to live a happy, fulfilled life—no matter the challenges swirling around us these days — through the ancient yogic teachings of Paramhansa Yogananda. With engaging and easy-to-read blogs including :Dealing with Change and Loss, Hope for a Better World, Keeping Your Balance, and Faith, Attunement, and Courage. The authors keep the spiritual journey lighthearted, simple, and down-to-earth.

More Selected Offerings